Get Ahead in Your New Job

Get Ahead in Your New Job

How to make an impact in the first 100 days

John Lees

 Open University Press

How to Get Ahead in Your New Job
How to make an impact in the first 100 days
John Lees

ISBN: 9781526847492
e-ISBN: 9781526847508

Published by McGraw-Hill Education
8th Floor, 338 Euston Road
London
NW1 3BH
UK

Telephone: +44(0) 20 3429 3400
Website: www.mheducation.co.uk

British Library Cataloguing in Publication Data
A catalogue record for this book is available from the British Library

Library of Congress Cataloguing in Publication Data
The Library of Congress data for this book
is available from the Library of Congress

Senior Commissioning Editor: Hannah Kenner
Editorial Assistant: Karen Harris
Content Product Manager: Ali Davis

Typeset by Transforma Pvt. Ltd., Chennai, India

Printed in Great Britain by Bell and Bain Ltd, Glasgow

PRAISE FOR *GET AHEAD IN YOUR NEW JOB*

"At a time where people move jobs with greater frequency this is an area many truly underestimate. I have seen many people simply roll from old organisation into new without enough thought around their new responsibilities, establishing the right relationships and being clear on what good looks like in the first 3 months. This book will not only improve your impact in your current role but will reshape your career. A great read."

Graham Lucas, Managing Director, Michael
Page Recruitment Specialists

"All John's books are easy to read and packed with really practical advice and insights. The focus this time is how to effectively 'on board' into a new role and/or organization. As an HR leader one of my key goals is to attract and retain the talent we need to be successful. One of the main challenges I find is to help people realise their potential, acclimatize to the culture and feel they can be themselves too. I think this book is a great resource to aid this journey starting from the first interview, reducing the time to optimal effectiveness and help people feel happier in their new role. I strongly recommend it."

Gordon McFarland Global HR Director
BCG Global Services

"How you start a new role matters – and never more so in a world where you're likely to change jobs (and careers) multiple times. This is an authoritative, comprehensive, but also practical guide to being more confident, more effective and, ultimately, more impactful in your new position."

Richard Alderson, founder of Careershifters

"John extends his inimitable and accessible style to the important topic of transitioning successfully to a new role. He puts the individual in the driving seat of the career management vehicle, and exhorts the reader to develop 'career awareness', being mindful of the desire for interesting work, the needs of the employer and ways to the best of the overlap. The several checklists in this book are invaluable."

Rob Nathan, Chartered Psychologist and co-author of Career Counselling (Sage)

"John provides clear guidance in his latest book for business professionals at all levels, specifically when job-hunting and navigating the first 100 days and beyond in a new role/organisation. The book has surfaced many important questions from the HR/employer perspective, as to what more organisations should be doing to support the successful on-boarding of new hires. A highly thought-provoking read!"

Andrew Ktoris, Head of Talent for Simmons & Simmons, international law firm

"Many career books focus up to the point an offer is accepted. It's assumed that everyone will know what to do from that point onwards. If you ignore the importance of the first few months in a role, whether it's a new company, a different part of an existing

employer or even a simple promotion, the chances of success can be seriously compromised. John Lees' advice for the first 100 days (and beyond) is highly practical and invaluable to job-seekers at any level. I only wish his book had been available on the numerous occasions I've changed jobs myself."

Martin Goodwill, CEO, Great People Inside Ltd

PRAISE FOR *HOW TO GET A JOB YOU LOVE*

"This book is a treasure. Read it, devour it, use it, and find that job you once dreamed about but had almost given up on."

Richard Nelson Bolles, author of What
Color Is Your Parachute?

"I frequently recommend job seekers or those at a career crossroads to read How to Get a Job You Love as it offers practical and easily accessible advice from someone with vast experience in the area."

Joëlle Warren MBE, DL, Executive Chair,
Warren Partners

"When I read John's writing, two things happen. First, I feel as if he's standing right there, personally advising me. And second, I always come away thinking over the issue in a new way. It's a rare and very useful, gift."

Sarah Green, Executive Editor,
Harvard Business Review

"This is THE definitive careers book which just keeps on getting better. I recommend it to listeners on my podcast and to my coaching clients, as it is up to date and provides clear, accessible and engaging career

guidance which will help readers no matter what stage they are in their job seeking journey. Life is too short to spend your time doing a job you don't enjoy. This book gives you the practical step-by-step skills, exercises and strategies you will need to get the job you'll love."

James Curran, Career coach and podcast
host at www.graduatejobpodcast.com

"Thank you John, for producing yet another How to Get a Job You Love masterpiece, now in its 10th edition. This latest edition combines John's extensive wisdom of the complex world of careers, with heaps of practical and accessible advice on enhancing your career prospects. With new features such as up to the minute advice on using social media in your job search, and fine-tuning your 'career narrative', this is a 'must-read' for anyone who wants to maximise their job satisfaction and explore the next step in their career."

Sophie Rowan, bestselling author of
'Brilliant Career Coach – How to Find
and Follow your Dream Career'

"For years, John Lees has been the smartest voice in career coaching. His insight and advice are a must-read for anyone entering today's competitive job market."

Rebecca Alexander, Dossier Editor,
Psychologies Magazine

"I know first hand the joy that being in the right career can bring and I commend John Lees for his books and seminars which help other people do just that."

Rosemary Conley CBE

To Christopher Lees

our amazing, funny, creative Mr Chris.

Contents

About the author

John Lees is one of the UK's best-known career strategists and the author of a wide range of business titles. *How to Get a Job You Love* regularly tops the list as the bestselling career change handbook by a British author and was twice selected as the WH Smith Business Book of the Month. John's wide range of career and business books have been translated into Arabic, Georgian, Polish, Japanese, and Spanish. In 2012, he wrote the introduction to the *Harvard Business Review Guide to Getting the Right Job*.

John has written careers columns for *Metro* and *People Management*. He appears frequently in the national press and his work has been profiled in *Management Today, Psychologies, Coaching at Work*, and *The Sunday Times*. Television appearances include *Back to Work* (BBC Interactive), *Working Lunch* (BBC2), *Dispatches* (Channel 4), *Talking Business* (BBC World), and *Tonight – How To Get A Job* (ITV). He has delivered career workshops in Australia, Germany, Ireland, New Zealand, Mauritius, Spain, South Africa, Switzerland, and several parts of the USA.

John is a graduate of the universities of Cambridge, London, and Liverpool, and has spent most of his career focusing on the world of work, spending 25 years training recruitment specialists. He is the former Chief Executive of the Institute of Employment Consultants (now the IRP) and an Honorary Fellow of the IRP.

He has consulted for a wide range of organisations, including: British Gas Commercial, The British Council, CIPD, Endsleigh, Gumtree, Harrods, Hiscox, The House of Commons, ICAEW, Imperial College, The Association of MBAs, Lloyds Banking Group, Marks & Spencer, the National Audit Office, Standard Life, Totaljobs, plus business schools across the UK. He served as Joint Chair of the Association of Career Professionals-UK (2011–13), was a founding Board Director of the Career Development Institute, and in March 2016 was elected a NICEC Fellow.

Alongside his day job, John works as an ordained Anglican priest in the Diocese of Exeter. He is a Prebendary of Exeter Cathedral and also serves as Bishop's Officer for Self-Supporting Ministry. John is married to the poet and children's writer Jan Dean.

John Lees Associates helps career changers in the UK and elsewhere. We specialise in helping people to make difficult career decisions – difficult either because they don't know what to do next or because there are barriers in the way of success.

w: www. johnleescareers.com
tw: @JohnLeesCareers
Facebook: www.facebook.com/JohnLeesCareers
LinkedIn: How To Get A Job You'll Love Network

Acknowledgements

With age comes, perhaps later than it should, a realisation of those many people I haven't thanked enough.

I'd like to express enormous gratitude to Becky Charman for managing my PR for many years with great energy, and to my agent James Wills at Watson, Little for his unstinting support. Thanks also to my editors Hannah Kenner and Caroline Prodger, and the whole team at McGraw-Hill, and of course to Kate Howlett, Managing Consultant at John Lees Associates, for all her encouragement and ideas.

I'm grateful to colleagues who have let me road-test ideas with different audiences: Mel Barclay and Adi Mechen (LHH Penna), Helen Walker (Bentley), Janice Chalmers (Surrey University Business School), James Curran (Graduate Job Podcast), Helen Collins (Careers Springboard Bracknell), Lindsay Comalie and Nicola Pogson (Imperial College), Liz Dimmock (Women Ahead), Andrew Ktoris (University of Birmingham), Lisa Jones (Officers' Association), Wendy Pearson (Durham University Business School), Sarah Jackson (Warwick Business School), Rob Nathan (CCS), Jessica Taylor-Delaney (PageGroup), Paul Thurston (AMBA), and Marie Zimenoff (Career Thought Leaders). I'm also in debt to the community of NICEC fellows for their collective wisdom.

Thanks to those people who over more than two decades have supported and informed my work: Will Beale, Gill Best,

Jo Bond, Jim Bright, Julian Childs, Hilary Dawson, Sara Dewar, Matthias Feist, Peter Fennah, Gill Frigerio, Helen Green, Ajaz Hussain, Esi Kpeglo, Stuart Lindenfield, Rosemary McLean, Stuart Mitchell, Derek Osborn, Carole Pemberton, Daniel Porot, Rhymer Rigby, Stuart Robertson, Valerie Rowles, Joëlle Warren, and Ruth Winden.

I take this moment to remember with gratitude two colleagues who are no longer with us. I'm thinking of my friend and publicist Sue Blake, and of course the inspirational teacher Richard Nelson Bolles, author of the world-famous *What Color Is Your Parachute?*, whose death in 2017 left a huge gap in the careers world.

Other careers books by John Lees published by McGraw-Hill Professional

How to Get a Job You Love **(2018, 10th edition)**
ISBN 9781526847140
This definitive career handbook now celebrates its twentieth year – designed to help anyone thinking, 'I want to do something different, but don't know what it is.'

'This book is a treasure.'
Richard Nelson Bolles, author of What Color is Your Parachute?

Knockout CV **(2013)**
ISBN 9780077152857
Building on an extensive review of what employers love and hate about CVs, this book helps you decide which CV format will work best for you, and reveals how to write CVs and cover letters that convey your strengths quickly and get you into the interview room.

Knockout Interview (2017)
ISBN 9780077189563

A definitive overview of the job interview process and how to prepare for it. Includes a wide range of example questions you will face, and strategies for how to answer them.

Career Reboot: 24 Tips for Tough Times (2010)
ISBN 9780077127589

Packed with quick-read, practical tips for rejuvenating your job search, this book is a must for anyone striking out in a difficult job market after redundancy or simply looking for new opportunities in a difficult market.

How to use this book

What will you achieve in your first three months in the role?

If you've been interviewed recently, you were probably asked this. It's a great question, pushing aside the claims you've made about your ability, and interrogating one key issue: what will you *do?*

Recruitment is an expensive process, and employers wonder how quickly new hires will provide a return on investment. Appointment decisions are made on the basis of compromise and uncertainty. Hiring organisations may find candidates impressive and may see useful evidence in their work history, but it's notoriously difficult to predict how people will actually perform on the job. Interviewers hope to find out by asking this full-on interview question about what you'll achieve in three months. Interviews for sales roles are sometimes more specific and exacting: 'What's your 30, 60, and 90 day plan?'

During shortlisting, interview, and the job offer phase, hiring managers judge candidates on their ability to provide assurances of short-term success. They tell external recruiters that they need someone who will 'hit the ground running'.

The question that lingers

Getting a job offer doesn't mean the question is parked. Even though you have a contract of employment, you're untested and under scrutiny, especially in your first few weeks in the role. From day one you're in the spotlight, being measured up. Consciously or unconsciously, colleagues are weighing up whether hiring you was a good decision (especially if your background is slightly unusual, or if you are an outside candidate given the job in preference to talented internal applicants).

Staff at various levels will be aware of early rumours about why you were given the job and what you seem to offer. Some are watching for early signs that confirm or undermine your interview promises. One or two colleagues are looking at you with a special perspective. If they took part in the decision to hire you, their reputation may be at stake. If you look and sound like an imposter, you put a dent in their reputation as well as your own.

There will be others in more senior roles, perhaps not directly involved in hiring you, but now responsible for decisions about your future. Even from the earliest point of contact, these senior staff may start to form conclusions about your future – speculating if you're a star, a plodder, or perhaps someone who won't be around for long.

If you think that all this assessing and performing is happening rather fast, you're right. Long, relaxed induction programmes – where employers took a month or more to help new hires settle in – are a thing of the past. Where at one time batches of staff attended formal events to help them learn about the organisation, gently easing staff into their new roles, today the expectation is that you learn fast and get on with the job. Some 'onboarding' still happens (see Chapter 2), but new appointees are generally expected to start getting results immediately – almost before they've been given an in-house email address.

This raised level of expectation doesn't just focus on sales jobs, managerial roles, or experienced staff; many entry-level appointments are offered on the same basis.

People commonly assume that transitioning your way into a new role is easier if you have extensive work experience. The opposite can often be true – having learned how to embed yourself in one work culture, it can be hard to move into another. Additionally, as an experienced candidate, your new role might have a significant impact on your CV. As someone with an established career history, you may feel the stakes are higher for you now than they were at the outset of your career.

100 days

Why so much attention to the first 100 days in a new role? Essentially, because this is a critical phase in an important new relationship. A small number of individuals in an organisation met you and were involved in the decision to hire you. A much larger audience will be looking for evidence to see if that decision was a good one.

Compared with internal staff, some of whom may have applied for the role, you're an unknown quantity. Decisions will be made very early about whether you fit in, whether you are good value for money, and whether you can deliver on the promises you've made. Even more importantly, people who matter are deciding whether you have a future inside the organisation.

The first 100 days you spend in a role are therefore vitally important to the way the role unfolds, and may be critical to your future success. Individuals who will make important decisions about your future may feel they have enough information at the end of that period to answer a key question: *are you up to the job?*

This rush to judgement may sound unreasonable. After all, some roles take years, not months, to master. However, in today's frenetic world of work, three months is a long time. Rather than planning to make an impression in the long term, it's safer to assume that the way you perform and interact with others will be noticed quickly, and assumptions are created or reinforced. Some of these assumptions will have long-term consequences. It's certainly no exaggeration to suggest that in many high-pressure environments, you need to deliver tangible, observed results in the first three months to have any long-term credibility.

So, are there things you can think about and do in order to hit the ground running? Most certainly.

This book has three aims:

1. to help you see the importance of your first 100 days in a new role;
2. to help you make the right kind of impact in those 100 days, taking care to manage your reputation; and
3. to help you build on these first three months in the job as part of a longer-term career plan.

This book will be helpful to you if you're about to start a new job, or if you're in your first 6–12 months and still trying to work out how to build key relationships and start to make an impact. It can also help you if you're about to accept a job offer.

Navigating the chapters ahead

Chapter 1 **Taking a new job for the right reasons** offers you a chance to interrogate a job offer and undertake 'due diligence', exploring the underlying reality of a role.

Chapter 2 **Getting a grip on your new role** explores some of the initial problems new staff experience where minimal support and communication are on offer, helping you to adopt more active career thinking.

Chapter 3 **Initial impact** underlines the importance of first impressions, exploring how to challenge expectations and assumptions.

Chapter 4 **The organisation and you** shows you how to decode the organisation, spotting the outcomes that make your contribution most effective, and ways of understanding the bigger picture.

Chapter 5 **Mapping the organisation** takes organisational analysis to a new level with a mapping tool that encourages you to learn more by reaching out to useful people.

Chapter 6 **Quick wins and slow burns** outlines some great ways to provide early results.

Chapter 7 **Managing key relationships** explores the need to build relationships of trust quickly, spotting people who can help or hinder progress.

Chapter 8 **Road blocks – difficult situations and people** looks at better ways of managing difficult conversations and relationships, as well as organisational politics.

Chapter 9 **How work reputations are built and shaken** helps you understand how your personal reputation is built in the first few months in the role.

Chapter 10 **Reinventing yourself** looks at situations where this initial reputation doesn't fit the way you would like your future to be shaped.

Chapter 11 **Career traps** reviews classic situations and actions which put limits on your future.

Chapter 12 **Surviving, thriving, and negotiating change** starts to take a longer-term perspective on your role and reveals how to get the most out of career conversations.

Chapter 13 **Review, build, and know when it's time to move on** helps you identify opportunities to develop your career and potentially think about your next move.

Part 1

The first 100 days

Taking a new job for the right reasons

'Diligence is the mother of good fortune.'
Miguel de Cervantes (1615)

This chapter helps you to:

- Research to discover if the role is a good fit and adds usefully to your work history
- Avoid wasting interview time checking the job out
- Undertake due diligence
- Take time to think and research before formally accepting an offer
- Negotiate elements of the offer, or job content
- Analyse a newly created job with care

Getting under the surface of a role

This book looks at the best way of making a start in a job. Researching the role is key – before and after your start date.

Some argue that it is impossible to understand a job until you have been in post for a few months. The problem is that this learning period overlaps exactly with the time you have to make a positive impact. The harder you scrutinise predictable elements in the job before starting, the better prepared you are for the unpredictable.

Success in a new role does not begin on day one. It begins with research – the digging you do to prepare for interview questions, consider a job offer, and the preparation you do before day one.

Interrogating a job means extracting information from a wide range of sources. Simply relying on a job description is clearly not enough, as these documents are often inaccurate. Even making judgements on the information presented at interview may be insufficient. Scrutinise the whole package – role content and job offer.

Doesn't this happen during the interview?

Job hunters are sometimes told they should treat an interview as a two-way conversation – the organisation probes you, and you ask penetrating questions before deciding if you want the job. This is a misunderstanding of the process. For you, an interview has one purpose: to move you forward, and ultimately to win you a job offer. Everything you bring to the conversation should focus on this outcome. Get a job offer, and then make a final decision about whether to accept it.

Trying to check the job out during the interview takes up valuable time when you could be pitching evidence. Additionally, any answers you receive will be largely unreliable. Hiring managers under pressure to fill roles often need to 'sell' the organisation. You will hear about attractive aspects, not the difficult or uninspiring parts of the job. If you ask about the organisational culture, the answer will probably be bland and positive.

More importantly, asking these questions is counter-productive. Questions designed to help you decide if you want the role often don't land well. They can make you sound uncertain, uncommitted, cagy. You sound like you see the organisation in a negative light, and you'll only take the job if nothing else materialises.

Just at the moment when an interviewer is edging towards making you the number one choice, you're introducing doubt into the conversation. Now the interviewer's attention jumps to a darker place, suddenly required to consider reasons the role might not suit you. For example, if you ask a cautious-sounding question about staff turnover, what an employer hears is the word 'but'. As in, 'I'm interested in the role, *but* I'm starting to have reservations . . .'.

Use interview questions to build your case

This advice does not mean you avoid asking questions. Failure to ask great questions signals a lack of preparation, as well as weak interest. Good questions show you've given the role a great deal of thought, and you already sound engaged and motivated.

Questions about the organisation or role are useful if they have one aim – to convince someone to make a positive decision about you. If you're asking a question about the future of the role, for example, you are doing so in order to create in the mind of the interviewer *a picture of you doing the job*. Once someone clearly visualises you doing the job, it's hard to say 'no'.

Do ask about the impact of the role, and its future. You will learn a little about the job, but that's a side benefit. The main reason for asking questions is to demonstrate fit, and to impress. Ask questions which enable you to showcase your experience. Well-researched, 'smart' questions (see Chapter 2) present opportunities for you to offer additional evidence matching you to the job.

Deal with doubts outside the interview room. Don't ask questions just to work out if you should take the job, as there are better ways of finding the answer to this puzzle.

Exploiting the gap

There is often a short gap between informal offer and your final acceptance. You may be under pressure to accept an offer immediately. However, the first offer is normally informal, and it usually takes an organisation a few days to produce a formal written job offer – longer where there are complicated contractual elements that must be negotiated with Human Resources or senior management. You may ask for clarification or changes. This window may be open for just 72 hours, a time when you should look hardest at the organisation. Even this small window of opportunity gives you the chance to answer the most important question: *Do I know enough about the role to accept it with confidence?*

It's perfectly reasonable to take a day or two to think about an offer, but again, avoid sounding negative. Make any response positive, even if you have private doubts. If your reaction to a written offer sounds like a list of niggling complaints, or like backtracking on things already agreed, then the relationship will start to cool. You may still get the job, but this initial shift in tone may have unintended, long-term consequences. If you create a sense that you were uncomfortable with the offer but accepted the role anyway, this shapes your reputation before you step foot in the building.

Continue the due diligence you began while job hunting. Even if you think everything about the job is perfect, it still pays to find out more about what you're taking on. Begin your background checks as soon as an offer is made.

But what kind of background checks? Talk to anyone who knows the organisation well. This will include anyone who has recently worked there as an employee or consultant, or industry contacts who know where the organisation sits in the marketplace. Talk to people who know the context and have no axe to grind. Try to get a sense of the unpublished agenda: What is the organisation really like?

What does it want to become? What does success look like in roles like the one you will be filling? How deliverable are the promises made to you about job content, responsibilities, and role development?

Due diligence

The employer has decided. Now it's your turn. It's time to make sure that the role on offer is a healthy working match – a good compromise between your preferences and what the organisation needs. You do this by undertaking 'due diligence' – in-depth, objective checks, similar to the way one organisation looks at another during a merger or acquisition. Having been impressed by the shiny paintwork, look under the bonnet.

Taking a permanent role adds a significant new chapter to your CV. During the next 10–15 years, you may find yourself explaining this job choice to recruiters, justifying why it seemed like a useful stepping stone. Taking a new role matters for more than 100 days – it may impact on your whole career.

Passively accepting a job offer without investigation is therefore risky. With a job offer in your hand you may feel flattered and grateful that the selection process is over. It's a mistake people make every day, putting vast amounts of energy into winning a job, and very little effort into two equally important stages: accepting the job, and starting the job.

Think about what you need, and compare this to what's on offer. On a surface level this means close attention to details of the offer. However important these parts of the deal are, they are less important than the real building blocks of the job – the challenges you will face, and the expertise you will gain.

If you're considering a job offer, use the **Due Diligence Checklist**. It will also provide a useful overview if you've recently started in a role.

Due Diligence Checklist

Look at the key ingredients in the role. Give each ingredient a score between 1 and 4, where:

1 = Not relevant/Not important
2 = Important to me, but not on offer
3 = Important to me, might be negotiable
4 = A strong match to what I'm looking for

Base salary	Other financial elements
Pension	Other financial benefits
Travel and nights away from home	Flexible working
Annual leave	Other non-financial benefits
Size of organisation	Size of team
Authority to make decisions	Budgets available
Relationship with boss	Team fit
Targets	Next appraisal/review date
Promotion prospects	Job security
Main challenges	Opportunities for learning
Variety	Status, responsibility
Impact on my CV	Organisational culture and values
Opportunities for extending my network	Community/charity involvement
Other (define your own):	

Add to the end of the Due Diligence Checklist any other ingredients that matter to you. This checklist naturally also points you to questions – further things you need to find out about the job. It will reveal job components that are important, and those which are deal-breakers.

Look at the items that you gave a score of 2. Can you manage without them? Look at the items you scored 3. Which do you plan to ask about and negotiate? (Even if you've started the role, you may get a chance to consider these again in a future review.)

Dig deeper

Due diligence begins when you send in your CV, and goes up a gear following a job offer. Aim to find out *why the role exists* – the problems it solves, and where it fits into the organisation. This gets beneath the gloss and the detail, and helps you predict how your performance will be judged in the short and long term.

Many roles involve tough targets, but you need to be sure what this role requires – in concrete terms. Some job descriptions are exact in their targets, others are ambitious statements. Be clear what reality you're looking at. What's the track record of other team members? If you're expected to achieve significant results rapidly, or force changes which the organisation has struggled to implement in the past, look hard at support you will be given and the things that will get in the way.

Watch the tone of your response to the organisation

We touched above on the way that asking apparently doubtful interview questions can bounce badly, making you sound indifferent or cold. While you're negotiating a job offer, watch the temperature of your responses.

If you're asking for adjustments to the offer (which could range from the pay deal to job content), offer them in a 'happy sandwich'. Bearing in mind that listeners focus on the first and last thing you say, pack a negative inside two positives. Begin by expressing delight that you've been offered the role. *Briefly* mention the things you'd like to discuss further. Then close by turning up the warmth again, saying how you looking forward to starting. Major positive, minor negative, major positive – a happy sandwich.

For example, request changes to a job description in a phone call like this: *I was over the moon when I read your offer letter. I know there are a few details we're sorting out, but I wonder if we could talk a little more about one area – my client responsibilities? I've got a few ideas I'd like to send you by email. Perhaps we can talk later today? Great – I'm really looking forward to starting the job.*

If your natural style is reserved rather than effusive, rehearse your happy sandwich aloud before picking up the phone. Introverts often get into difficulties here because their natural style tends to make them sound more cautious than they really feel.

Negotiation – if you don't ask . . .

It's easy to assume that it's risky to try to negotiate a job offer, or it looks pushy. However, some candidates know that an offer is the first stage in a negotiation process.

One mistake that candidates make is to assume that job content is non-negotiable. Some roles are well-planned or rigid in their structure, and in these cases you may not get very far. However, many jobs are fluid at the point they are offered, reflecting the pace of change or uncertainty about how the organisation wants the role to develop.

Look at small changes that would improve job content for you, perhaps expanding on the skills you will acquire. If the job content isn't right, and that's a deal breaker for you, make a reasoned argument. For example, if the organisation is about to fill another vacancy in your team and the new role diminishes yours, ask for a rethink. Do certainly push back if there are ingredients you'd like to add if they fit two criteria: (a) they make the job more interesting *and* (b) they will allow you to make a greater impact.

Tipping the balance

Why discuss this now? Simple – leverage. In terms of job content (a conversation that begins 'I'd like to talk about ways you can get more value out of my experience'), you probably have more influence, more leverage at the job offer stage than you will have for another 18 months.

At this point, you can almost certainly negotiate at least one thing to your advantage. Once an organisation has decided to make you an offer, there is a high degree of psychological commitment – plus a perceived opportunity cost if you walk away. They've decided they want you for the role, and don't want to go through the pain and cost of having to rethink and re-advertise.

Employers are prepared to fix things in order to bring you on board; however, once you are settled in a role, an organisation expects you to start achieving. Going back to a senior manager six months after starting to talk about job content sounds like a mismatch, and conveys enough disappointment to risk setting yourself up to fail.

Don't try to negotiate more than a handful of elements in an offer. You can push back on two or three things that matter to you. This might be about an improved pay deal, or possibly about fringe benefits. It might be about access to learning, or the support available to you, or flexible working. One important area of negotiation which may continue after your start date is to understand what an organisation really requires of you. You'll get part of the answer now, and more at your first review.

Ask for a visit

Due diligence shouldn't be a paper exercise alone. In addition, ask for a chance to come alongside your new colleagues while the details of the written offer are being finalised. This mustn't sound as if you're saying, 'I'm not sure about this role'. It needs to sound more like 'while we're sorting out the paperwork, I'd love to spend some time with the team'.

You'll probably be talking to people you haven't met yet, so this can be enormously rich in information. You start to get a real sense of team 'chemistry', where your skills and experience will fit in, and whose toes you might be treading on by accepting the role. You also may discover something about the working style of your colleagues and the culture of the organisation. Finally, it's always helpful to get some sense of the how long the last post holder was in the role.

Don't be afraid of asking for some time with new colleagues while you are still processing a job offer. If you're communicating with the right tone, most organisations see this as a sign of your commitment and an easy way of beginning the onboarding process. If an organisation says 'no', this might be for valid reasons such as business confidentiality. If the organisation refuses without any reasonable explanation, this could be a danger sign that there are hidden problems.

What happens if you discover negative information during your site visit? Like any negative information you pick up, cross-check with other opinions. Websites such as glassdoor.com provide insights into organisational culture, but beware of the inherent bias of much online material – there is inevitably extensive sounding-off from disgruntled employees, and more negative than positive opinion. Ask around for a more rounded picture. External recruiters will sometimes give an opinion about an organisation, but they may be discreet if they are hoping to place you there.

Look most closely at staff turnover. How many of the people in your department were there two years ago? How long do people stay, typically? Why do they move on? Those organisations that hang on to committed and motivated people generally have healthy working cultures. Also, ask about movements of key and senior staff. Who has arrived recently? Who is likely to move on or retire soon?

An interrogative start

Some of this chapter looks at questions you should ask before accepting an offer. Much of this advice is also helpful if you have already started a job.

Even after your first few weeks, you're still working hard to understand your role and the organisation it sits in, and to recognise the extent of your 100-day challenge. You may have been in the role for months, but the principles are the same – find out more, learn quickly, focus on the things that matter. In order to get ahead, you need to get your head round the problems you face.

Look ahead at the way the job is likely to develop, opportunities for learning, and the chances of progression. Exploring the role in depth means understanding the people you will be working with, and how likely it is you will fit in. The headlines are set out in the **Job Start Checklist** below.

Job Start Checklist

1. *The role*

- Are you clear about the main focus of the job? What will you be doing most of the time?
- Is this a new job? If so, is it clear what the duties are, and how much will need to be negotiated as the job develops?
- Are there goals or targets, and are they achievable? What are the consequences if they are not achieved?
- What learning opportunities can you negotiate at the job offer stage?
- What changes to the job description would you like to negotiate at this stage?
- How much of the job is routine? How long will the role keep you interested?
- How far does the job present new challenges? Variety? How much will it stretch you?
- How is the job likely to change in the next year or two?
- Is this a reasonably good role to add to your CV? How will you explain the decision to take this job in five years' time?
- What induction training and support is on offer? How quickly before you are expected to work independently?

2. *The organisation*

- Who will you be working for most of the time? What signs suggest that this will be a good working relationship?
- What are your colleagues like? How long before you fit into the new team?
- Have you seen tangible evidence of organisational values and culture in action?
- Have you spent any time at all with the people you will actually be working with?
- What is the organisation's track record on staff retention?
- How long was the previous job holder in the role?

When the role is brand new

Take care with a newly created role. Here your enquiries need to be more exacting. You might have a wonderful opportunity to write your own script, or you might face unexpected problems. You may fail without knowing why, particularly if the role wasn't designed with care. Find out why the new role has been created, and why it wasn't needed before. Problems with newly created roles occur around *planning* and *permission.*

Probe the *planning* that went into the creation of this newly minted post. Questions about targets, deliverables, and blocks to progress are vital – they will give you insights into how far the organisation has thought about the role. Sometimes a new job starts as a great idea but job content becomes confused by cross-departmental disputes.

Look also at *permission.* Will you be allowed to do what you're asked to do? Where the role heads up a new project or implements big changes, research hard. Get a sense of whether the organisation is really committed to the idea. How embedded is the change set out in the role? Have key players indicated their buy-in? Find out if the right backing exists to allow you to make the changes envisaged.

If your job seems to be about implementing change, find out what drives that change and whether senior players are committed to it. On many occasions talent is brought in to implement changes that the organisation is not ready for – or only partially committed to. So another great question to ask your background contacts is, 'how seriously does the organisation believe in this job?'

'Must do' list

- ✓ Learn how to understand your new job and why you were hired to fill it.
- ✓ Perform due diligence on a role, even if you're happy to accept it.
- ✓ If you're still processing a job offer, seek clarification on job content and attempt to negotiate it where this matters to you.
- ✓ Otherwise, negotiate a small number of elements in the offer.
- ✓ If possible, visit the organisation before you finally accept an offer, especially if you have concerns about the work culture.
- ✓ Take particular care to understand expectations and constraints if the job is a new role.
- ✓ Interrogate using the Job Start Checklist, even if you started in the role some time back.

2

Getting a grip on your new role

'Find out what you like doing best, and get someone to pay you for doing it.' **Katharine Whitehorn (1975)**

This chapter helps you to:

- Understand why the first 100 days in a new role are so critical
- Recognise that you need to plan actively rather than passively hope the organisation will give you a soft landing
- Consider your impact in the context of a rapidly changing economy
- Begin a new role as you mean to go on
- Reconsider career planning and learn the skill of 'career awareness'
- Move from passive to active career behaviours

The critical Q1

We judge performance in a number of ways. Many organisations look at income and expenditure on a quarterly basis – Q1, Q2 . . .. As you get to grips with your new role, you are under equal scrutiny. However, for you, Q1 is what matters. By the end of your first 100 days, you can make a strong set of impressions on people who will influence your future – they will promote you, advance opportunities in your direction, or recommend you.

It might feel both arbitrary and abrupt to make decisions about new staff members within such a limited time frame. There is a great deal to learn – about operating procedures, key relationships, and culture – and sometimes a great deal of knowledge to be absorbed before you become proficient. Fitting into a new culture often requires a great deal of concentrated attention to relationship building and 'decoding' (see Chapter 4).

This 100-day window is important because of simple psychology: first impressions. Human brains are hard-wired to judge within micro-seconds if someone new is a potential threat or an ally. We unconsciously decide within minutes whether we find someone easy to get on with. This probably matters even more to us with newcomers to an organisation. No one is surprised to hear a conversation at the coffee machine beginning, 'What do you think of the new team leader?'

This first set of impressions (see Chapter 3) can strongly influence subsequent decision-making. Impressing a senior manager with a good question or helpful piece of information may ultimately push a promotion in your direction, or ensure that your name comes up at the right time. Showing that you have good questions but you're not immediately pushing ideas forward can reap benefits many months down the line.

These early judgements are about whether someone new fits into our 'tribe'. That's the critical factor in your first 100 days – fitting in is far more important than impressing.

100 days

Why 100 days, not 90 days or 110 days? Why not plain old 'three months'? Largely because our culture uses 100 days as a threshold – a point where it's clear if you're winning or losing. Napoleon, returned from exile in 1815, survived just 100 days until his defeat at Waterloo. US presidents are judged on what they achieve in the same time frame. Franklin Roosevelt, in his first 100 days, pushed 15 significant bills through Congress. Commentators also point out that he only achieved this result by rapidly building a relationship with Congress. President John F. Kennedy announced ambitious plans in his inaugural address, adding that these things would not be finished within his first 100 days. President Trump announced his 100-day record as 'historic'. It has become a universal time frame in politics and business for measuring impact, and whether people live up to their promises.

Problems of onboarding

You've got a job offer and a start date. Job done! *Or is it?*

It's interesting how often people sleepwalk their way into a new job, accepting what's on offer and asking no further questions. After all, there is something in the way an organisation handles you that says 'leave it to us'. You will be moved around like a parcel on induction training, familiarisation tours, and learning events.

Of course, this assumes that you will experience an effective induction. In the past, organisations offered structured, often lengthy induction programmes – frequently involving a familiarisation tour of the premises, briefing meetings, and an introduction to a wide range of people. Today, organisations still talk about 'onboarding', and yet the process seems to be suffering some neglect. At its best, a well-structured onboarding process includes initial coaching, extensive support, and an early review meeting. Often it's a whistle-stop tour followed by an assumption that you will get on with the job.

A 2017 Gallup survey (O'Boyle and Harter, n.d.) suggested that only 12 per cent of employees strongly agree their organisation does a great job of onboarding new workers. The report suggested that where a good working relationship is not established quickly, retention problems often follow. It seems clear that some organisations consistently fail to deliver on the promises they made during recruitment, and make such a poor job of onboarding that key staff move on within a short period. The US-based Work Institute published a report (2018) which suggested that one in three employees would likely leave their jobs in the next three years, and 40 per cent would leave within their first year at a company.

So, if organisations can't commit optimum levels of time to onboarding you, and the expectation is that you shouldn't need it anyway, what's your plan?

Starting as you mean to go on

Using this book, decide *how* you're going to hit the ground running. This means benchmarking yourself against the role all over again, just as you did at interview. What do you need to learn about? What key people do you need to meet quickly? Which part of the job description are you still uncertain of? It's clearly vital to have a clear understanding of your job.

You undertook a lot of research into the role to win a place on the shortlist and to shine during the interview process. Keep control by looking at the way you prepare to start the job. The process of investigation needs to continue well beyond day one, providing you with a clearer picture of the scope of the organisation, its history, brands, market reputation, along with its key locations, main products and services, and its important personalities. When you discover how much there is to find out, you identify vital questions that will fuel your early conversations.

The ground work

To learn about your new organisation, start by looking at the things it puts front and centre in its shop window. A great shortcut to do this is to look at the organisation's online media pages, reading recent press releases, articles, and published research. Understanding the messages your employer has spent time and money broadcasting to the outside world gives you a very clear indication of its priorities.

Nothing communicates lack of commitment to a new role as a failure to undertake basic homework. This homework doesn't need to be confined to desk research. Showing genuine curiosity communicates commitment; demonstrating enthusiasm for a shared purpose is a great way of building new relationships.

Curiosity is best shaped by 'smart' questions – intelligent, well-informed questions that go to the heart of an issue and show you've already read a great deal about the organisation. In your questions, focus most intensely on products, projects, and outcomes that people are clearly proud to talk about. Learn about the jobs people do, and how they are performed. Discover how jobs mesh together. Start to work out which parts of the organisation run effectively, and those which are noticed most.

How far does your new role fit your career plan?

Most people seem to associate the word *career* with movement. They buy books when they need to write a CV or prepare for interviews. This is rather like only caring for your car the week before an MOT test. Your career is something that matters all the time. It needs regular reviews, updates, audits. Occasionally, it will need a retune. Once or twice in a working life you may seek refreshment, wanting to do something very different.

The second big assumption is that many people have a detailed career plan. In fact, many careers are unplanned – created around a mix of chance and opportunity. It's arguable that work is now changing so fast that it seems impossible to plan 12 months ahead (see below for thinking about managing your career in an uncertain world). Even if a long-term plan seems out of your grasp, the steps you take in the first few months in a role can potentially have a huge impact on your future. So, getting ahead in your new job is one of the most effective ways of managing your career.

Adopting *career awareness*

Our traditional picture of career planning is having a long-term, step-by-step blueprint for how our working lives will shape up. Since professionals are trained to plan ahead and manage projects, we assume that a solid career plan should have a long-term trajectory. If this seems complicated, that's the point. Having concluded that such a plan is impossible to construct, we allow ourselves to drift.

Consider a more flexible, more accessible idea. *Career awareness* offers something rather different. It doesn't depend on luck or job change, but takes a snapshot of your current situation and choices.

Career awareness – the three vital questions:

1. What kind of work do I find interesting and a useful challenge?

2. What does my current (or next) employer *really* need?
3. How can I exploit the overlap, or create one?

Career awareness begins with these three vital questions, and keeps the next 18 months constantly in view. Rather than having a vague career plan at the back of a drawer, it's about being alert on something like a weekly basis to possibilities where you can match opportunities as they present themselves to your own career needs. This enables a new approach.

First, you understand what works for you. Not your ideal or perfect role, but one where you are engaged most of the time in work you find stimulating. There is a great deal in this book to help you (see Chapter 13, and for an in-depth review of your skills, values, motivation, and career thinking, see *How to Get a Job You Love*).

Second, you start to develop good personal radar – the ability to identify opportunities as they arise and to understand the needs of organisations. Improving your radar isn't just about being alerted to vacancies, but being in tune with organisations and sectors, spotting trends, and tracking down useful people. Identifying opportunities means keeping your ear to the ground, maintaining information networks, and retaining lifelong curiosity. You learn how to live within a role, perform well, but also add to it and build from it. It's about a continual process of review, on the hoof.

The third stage of career awareness is *matching* – where you have a clear picture of yourself and compare it with job-shaped opportunities. You will make active connections between what you have to offer and the needs of organisations.

So, consider your career as a rolling 18-month programme. Eighteen months is a useful time scale – long enough to adapt, acquire new skills, get to know a business or division in detail, and long enough to build networks and relationships.

As you get used to the idea you might think about a slightly longer game – the role you want to hold in 5 or 10 years' time. Long-term planning is not always impossible or irrelevant. If you're aiming at a board-level position, you will need to add key job titles and organisations to your CV.

Career awareness is therefore about really understanding yourself (your working style, preferred skills and contexts, what motivates you) and developing a linked awareness of what's going on around you in the organisation (see Chapters 4 and 5 for understanding your organisation better). Inevitably, you will also seek a wider sense of how your work sector is changing. This enhanced awareness of self and organisation leads to the next stage: matching yourself to new opportunities as they arise.

Career management: passive and active

How active or passive are you in your career decision-making? How much does your future depend on the intervention of others – your boss, your colleagues, or Human Resources? Research from the Institute for Employment Studies (2013) explored the thinking styles we adopt when making career decisions. For some, decisions are exploratory – ideas are tested out and choices made after reflection. Other people are more impulsive, responding with little thought to opportunities as they arise. Some decision styles are passive – taking the first job that comes along, or expecting an organisation to arrange all training and promotion opportunities. Passive approaches are highly vulnerable to the opinions of other people, such as when a young person is encouraged to work in the public sector because of outdated assumptions of job security and a good pension.

Becoming aware of passivity and challenging its impact is a vitally important step in career management:

Passive behaviours

- Assuming that someone else will manage your career for you.
- Waiting for the organisation to offer you opportunities for development.
- Assuming that you will be told when it's time to move up or change the focus of your role.
- Relying on the organisation to think about your learning objectives.
- Waiting for internal roles to be advertised or for a manager to recommend you for a new role.
- Expecting others to decode your work history to identify transferable skills.
- Only refreshing your CV when you look for a new job.
- When you move on, applying only for advertised roles, or expecting a recruitment consultancy to manage every aspect of transition.

As you can see, these behaviours are characterised by a lack of planning, a knee-jerk response to changing circumstances and a reliance on other people to push you in the right direction.

Active behaviours build on an understanding that a career is something to be monitored, even when things are going well. It's something to be tweaked and adjusted as you move forward. In this respect, it's rather like your skill set. You don't learn something new in January and then forget about your personal development until the end of the calendar year.

Active behaviours

(a) Starting a new job

- Obtain maximum information about expectations attached to your role.

- Gather information about the organisation you work for well outside your induction period.
- Build relationships with internal and external players who might influence your future.
- Take particular care to demonstrate the right behaviours, attitude, and results in the first three months in a role.
- Ask for an early review to check if you are meeting expectations.

(b) Longer term

- Find a mentor who can give you independent feedback and advice about the way you fit into an organisation or sector.
- Review your career, CV, and LinkedIn profile at least twice a year.
- Benchmark your skills and knowledge against others in similar roles, and seek learning to fill any evident gaps.
- Only go back to the job market when you're ready to evidence your strengths and achievements and have a good reason for moving on.

Other people will influence, guide, and open doors for you – but no one else will live out your experience. Taking control is a life-enhancing moment. Doing so right now, when you're starting a new job, means you're deciding that one person is in charge of the next phase of your working life – you!

Making your mark in turbulent times

If you haven't quite got used to the idea of taking active control, you're not alone. Just a few generations back, the idea that you had career choices was outside most people's experience. When employers offered long-term job security and relatively well-funded pensions in exchange for worker loyalty, the broad assumption was that employers did your career thinking for you. Training, promotion, welfare – these were under the organisation's control. This psychological contract began to dissolve in the late twentieth century in a new climate of acquisitions, mergers, and 'rightsizing'. In reality, the balance between employee independence and employer paternalism and control is something that often changes.

We have had several decades of organisations learning how to get more out of their resources and manage with leaner structures. This culture is now overlaid with a new reality: market unpredictability verging on chaos. World markets have been disrupted by a wide range of factors, including anxiety about international trading and the threat of trade wars, data insecurity, and the impact of climate change.

All this has happened alongside rapid developments in technology. When the average employer has little idea what kind of business it will be in 12 months' time, it needs staff who can deliver now, not two quarters down the line. Making a quick impact is now the norm rather than something seen just in exceptional candidates.

Deepening market insecurity has made the situation more complex. A number of organisations that have made very solid talent management offers have had to revise or retract them. Traditional business models of developing staff today who may be the leaders and high performers of tomorrow have been disrupted. Organisations are still using the language of hiring and retaining talent, but offers of long-term career enhancement appear over-optimistic.

A new psychological contract?

We may well be moving into a time where organisations are more honest and transparent about appointments – not necessarily offering fixed-term contracts, but talking more explicitly about short-term career 'deals'. Rather than thinking about 'permanent' appointments in the traditional sense, they may explicitly seek skills and knowledge they plan to bring into the business for 18-month projects.

We have had a great deal of time to get used to the mantra 'there are no jobs for life'. We might soon be hearing 'no job guarantee is valid for more than five years'.

The time you give to work

Think about the time and energy you put into work. You may be wondering if you can cover even half of the objectives set out for your role and still have time for sleep, let alone a life outside work.

We have an ever-changing attitude to the time we give to work. Only some three or four generations back people worked at least six days a week, often from dawn to dusk. In the last few decades, we've become mildly obsessed by the idea of work/life balance, and this usually means working shorter hours, retiring while boasting good health, and spending time on non-work activities.

During the twentieth century, there were many predictions of shorter working hours. In the 1980s, society seemed to be planning for a world where people retired early and had a great deal of leisure time. Since then we have switched to a 'long hours' work culture. Working life is continually being transformed by communications technology. Many workers feel a non-contractual obligation to read and respond to email and text messages outside working hours. Others take work home with them or go to the office at weekends.

We seem to want to live in the fast and slow lane simultaneously – working long hours in the office (and outside it) and at the same time talking and thinking about work/life balance. In 2019, several UK organisations announced they were switching to four-day work weeks to improve productivity. Workers in other parts of the economy are holding down more than one job to make ends meet.

We edge ever closer to circumstances familiar to those working in the legal and financial sectors, something pretty close to 24/7 working. In most families, at least one adult is working longer hours than they were a generation ago. It often feels as if there just aren't enough hours in the day to meet targets, attend meetings, and answer a constant barrage of emails.

Why consider working hours and time pressure in the context of a new role? First, reflection time may be in short supply as you cope with the pressures of a new role. You may find yourself extraordinarily busy, and lose a sense of the best place to apply your energy. Second, time pressure can mean that you neglect to look at your career as a big picture. When you accept a role, you think about what it adds to your CV. As you begin a role you should, as this book suggests, be thinking about visibility, career enhancement, and avoiding making a negative impression in the critical opening weeks.

Work consumes a great deal of your stamina and life energy. Your life may be divided roughly into three kinds of activity (paid work, leisure and chores at home, and sleep). After leaving full-time education, most of your best energy, imagination, and concentrated effort will go into work. Work will absorb a great deal of you, so decisions you make about your career are vitally important life decisions.

Choosing the kind of work you do, thinking carefully about career stages and decisions, and making the best of each new role – all are critical turning points. If you find that work consumes the best of your energy and attention, then choosing the work you do is one of life's most important decisions.

'Must do' list

- ✓ Keep a notebook to record what you take away from this book and actions you plan to take.
- ✓ Take your first 100 days seriously, making the most of them in terms of first impressions.
- ✓ Even if you've been in the role more than three months, use the strategies in this book to learn more about your organisation and how you fit in it.
- ✓ Think about where you have demonstrated *career awareness* in the past, and how you can use it to make the most of your new role.
- ✓ Consider your new role as part of a wider career plan.
- ✓ Review – where have you been passive in your career so far? How can you be more active?

3

Initial impact

'We don't know where our first impressions come from or precisely what they mean, so we don't always appreciate their fragility.' **Malcolm Gladwell (2006)**

This chapter helps you to:

- Manage the impression you make on others in your opening months in the role
- Disrupt the narrative of your starting reputation
- Spot allies, blockers, and career influencers
- Find out about the history of your role
- Consult, learn, and communicate quiet authority
- Rediscover why you were hired

Into the lion's den

Starting a new role will often be a stressful experience. Research published by www.jobsite.co.uk claimed that 20 per cent of people think the first day in a new job is scarier than many of life's most daunting events, including relationship problems, taking a driving test, having a baby, getting married, or telling your parents a well-kept secret (McCormick, 2007).

Getting a job offer is not the final stage of the process. Now you've got to begin the much more complicated task of convincing an employer that hiring you was a good decision. This decision won't be put to rest in your first week at work.

If you feel there's a lot at stake, you're right. Your first two weeks in the job may have far more impact on your image and prospects than any other fortnight you spend in the role. First impressions are formed – and they can have long-term effects. Day one is like a screen test – a few seconds of action are used to decide whether you fit the role. It's very difficult to alter a bad first impression. From the first handshake people are deciding whether your appointment was a good decision.

Avoid hitting the ground limping

New starters are often told they need to make an impact from their very first day. That's not easy. A new job presents a complex and sometimes overwhelming mass of information to decode – organisational jargon and systems, who does what, and how far you can implement the things you said you were able to do at interview.

Hitting the ground running in the wrong way might in fact be a career-limiting action (see Chapter 11). Pushing too hard and too quickly may confirm negative assumptions that are floating around even before you arrive. Your CV or background may already suggest to people that you have been hired as a new broom, and they may assume your aim will be to make their life uncomfortable.

Some of your colleagues may therefore have defence mechanisms already in place, such as the idea that your experience is irrelevant, or you don't know enough about the organisation to make good judgements. They may even wonder if you can do the job competently. Even relatively open-minded colleagues might be suspicious of someone who seems willing to change everything without really understanding what's working – and what isn't.

Your reputation starts before you do

When you start a role, you begin in a context – a set of prejudices and assumptions already made about you.

Where do these ideas come from? Many come from the hiring process. Small pieces of information gathered at this stage are being put together. Recruiting organisations rely on the 'radar' of staff who met you when you were on the premises attending interviews – not just interviewers, but also receptionists, security guards, and anyone you met on your walk-around. They will be asked for their impressions, before you're offered the job, and again when you have a start date. All kinds of people check in with these colleagues trying to work you out.

This reputational starting point is sketchy, based on loose evidence, and represents all kinds of hidden agendas. You might already be described as someone who wants to shake things up. If your background is outside the norm, colleagues might already be suggesting that an internal appointment would have been safer. You have only limited control over your starting reputation, as it's based on things you have little influence over – so far.

Being in the wrong mode

It's possible to start a new job in the wrong gear – job-hunting mode. When you're looking for a job you showcase your strengths, qualities, know-how, and the high points of your career. If this leads to a strong market reputation, you are recommended and shortlisted. This evidence is what gets you a job offer.

When you begin the role, this approach gets in the way. Talking up your abilities can often be inappropriate and counterproductive. Pushing yourself forward as if you're still in the selection process can easily play to expectations that you might be better at answering interview questions than doing the job.

How you've been looking for a job, and how you negotiated your new role, can both impact on your starting reputation. It's easy to assume that the way you've come across while job hunting is what you will be like when your feet are under the desk. If you've impressed by showcasing your achievements, it may be assumed that this is what you do all the time.

Your starting reputation might also be shaped by the way you negotiated the job offer. Candidates frequently have robust conversations about their side of the deal. And why not? Your employer may be specifically hiring you to negotiate tenaciously in the face of opposition, and should value these skills. However, if you pushed back hard when negotiating the job, it may be assumed that you're uncompromising or self-centred when working.

On the other hand, a meek approach to handling the job offer can have the opposite effect. If you passively accepted everything in the job offer including a slightly lower salary than you were expecting, this may be an indication that you are unlikely to fight your corner in difficult situations.

First base assumptions

As we've established, your reputation starts before you do. Even before you've been handed your security badge, a narrative is forming about who you are and whether you are a good fit. How you behave when people meet you confirms or challenges these expectations.

Your new colleagues may expect you to be a self-promoter because you sold your experience hard at interview. There may be suspicions that you intend to disrupt things, imposing your personality, introducing rapid change and new ways of working. Your direct reports may already be planning their self-protective lines of defence and blocking tactics.

Organisations are sometimes interested in hiring candidates with external experience. This may start working against you right now – your colleagues may see your lack of industry knowledge as a failure to understand their problems. They may be eager to discover hidden signs of incompetence.

Disrupt the narrative

Disrupting the narrative means challenging assumptions before they are set in stone, giving yourself time to adapt and fit in. When you're chasing down a job offer, you're in broadcast mode, getting your best points across. In your first day of work, turn the tables on these assumptions. Use surprise as your primary strategy.

Rather than listing your past achievements, switch your focus onto the track record of the team you're joining. Ask questions designed to draw out evidence of other people's skills and know-how. Listen to answers with attention. High-quality listening can make another person feel as if they are completely at the centre of your attention for a few moments. It's the same high-focus attentiveness exhibited by business leaders.

Instead of immediately bringing your ideas to the table and attempting to begin a process of change, show a willingness to learn. Demonstrate interest in – and respect for – the way things are done already. It's too glib to offer your past as the perfect solution to the organisation's future – ingrained problems are often more complex than they seem. Don't try to shake the tree in your first month. You really don't have enough information at your fingertips, even if you have been specifically hired to do this.

In other words, give your ego a holiday – put aside the evidence you've been using to convince other people to offer you the job. Stop broadcasting, and start listening. These opening days in a new job are a vital chance to build long-term relationships, so ask great questions without jumping in immediately with matching solutions based on your CV.

Getting back, temporarily, into interview mode

There is one important exception to the above advice. Shortly after you start you may meet a senior manager. The conversation may simply be a welcome, pointing you to resources and people you will find helpful.

However, sometimes the conversation takes you back to the interview room, especially where the senior player in front of you wasn't part of the selection decision. Curiosity or doubt might prompt demanding questions: 'What are your priorities?', or 'Tell me what ideas you're bringing to the role.'

In these circumstances, the interview is re-opened. You are, effectively, facing the 100-day question all over again. So in these circumstances, answering 'I'm here to learn' won't fly. Talk concisely about things from your past which you plan to draw on, strategies you intend to apply. Pitch at least one solid suggestion for a new project or working methods. Get that evidence across, see how it lands, and then use the opportunity to ask good questions about strategy and resources.

Consult, absorb, and share

Talk to people about the way they do their jobs, what they enjoy about them, and get a sense of the high and low points of their roles. Find out how they think about the products and services they are engaged with. Listen for information about frustrations and evidence of things that block progress. Probe these areas of difficulty sensitively; you don't want to stir up negativity or look like you mistrust the organisation. However, it is useful to discover how people feel about what they do.

This consultative approach is not mainly about information, it's about building trust. If you show genuine interest in colleagues' work and opinions, and tactfully avoid imposing your ideas, you overcome any sense that you're going to make lives uncomfortable. Also, you discover the people who will help you do your job well. Try phrases like 'I'd love to know how you solve this problem', or 'I'm here to learn from you', or 'I'm interested to know how I can make your job easier.'

Before day one, your relationship has been with people who make hiring decisions. Now your relationship is with the people you will work alongside and manage, and staff who manage you. There's a lot of human decoding going on, and a lot to learn. Use a notebook to jot things down immediately after a discussion. When you're introduced to somebody, make a note of their name plus something that helps you to remember them – a personal connection always makes a follow-up conversation easier.

Soft landing

The art of a soft landing, therefore, is to change the pre-existing narrative. Don't say 'I'm here to turn everything upside down' unless you were specifically hired to upset people and disrupt relationships. In every other respect, dial it back. People have already decided how you are going to be, and you're going to shift their perspective.

The strategy is a mechanism for avoiding early failure. If colleagues are on your side, they are far less likely to sabotage you with missing or inaccurate information, and more likely to take a collegiate approach. You increase the chances of open and honest communication. There are ways you can influence and exert power while still being diplomatic. You might be asked for solutions, and an insecure person in the same situation might rush in with some half-baked ideas. If you indicate that you're still absorbing information and doing some thinking, that elevates your status as a problem-solver. Indeed, spending time listening to other people's stories rather than showcasing your own makes you look far more like a leader than a run-of-the-mill manager.

Ask questions about previous successes – projects and strategies valued by the organisation. This approach heightens the social aspects of work and diminishes the functional aspects. It shows you're human, easy to get on with, that you listen to other people's perspectives, seek feedback, and you're more willing to learn than to impose.

Spend time absorbing the language of the organisation, spotting the biggest problems and opportunities. Soak up organisational charts, remembering the names and job titles of people that matter.

Ask questions like 'how did you start that?', 'what made that a success?', and 'what prevents that working in the future?'. Failure is often inevitable when people don't know what success looks like. Moving towards success isn't just about having a shared vision, it often relies on persuading colleagues to open a treasure chest of information. They will do this, but only when they trust you enough.

Brokers, blockers, and enablers

Take time in the first few weeks of the job to work out the human impact of your role. Initial responses will often give this away. If you hear 'I'm so glad you're here' or 'we were desperately keen to fill this role as soon as possible', this might feel positive, but it can also be a warning of a large amount of work that is about to hit your desk before you've had a chance to learn where your role fits.

Look at the space you're stepping into. Who are you helping? Whose job is less pressurised because you're here? Whose toes are you treading on just by occupying the role? Who can help you complete tasks, and who can make your life a misery? Who holds the keys to the things you need? Identify people who can and will help you.

Start by seeking information *brokers*. Information brokers are often at the heart of useful networks, and gain job satisfaction from the information they share. Many are positive-minded, happy to help, seeing sharing as part of their role. Look for colleagues who see you as the missing piece of the jigsaw, or as a breath of fresh air. As you identify potential allies, find out how their concerns and ambitions impact on yours. Sometimes they respond best if they see a deal – they help you, but expect help in return. Exchanging favours honestly and openly can in fact be a great way of working, leading to useful tip-offs: 'thought you might like the heads-up'.

Blockers are the opposite. These are the gatekeepers, people who hold information and will only release it if it suits their agenda. Sometimes this reflects a 'silo' mentality: 'I'll look after my interests/my team/my customers, and everyone else can fend for themselves.' Blockers know about sabotage, and everything about timing — providing data the day after you need it. Explore carefully to identify people who will trip you up this way.

Enablers are a special kind of ally. They make your life easier by unlocking parts of your role. An enabler might be someone you rely on for data or regular updates, the print room manager, or the IT specialist. Enablers will sometimes help if you respect and comply with their requirements.

Find out how their concerns and needs impact on yours. If procedures seem odd or flawed, run with them temporarily.

So, find out who will build you up, and who will pull you down. Key people come in different shapes and sizes, and may be very senior or very junior. Sometimes having a good relationship with the reception or security team makes life easier. Ask colleagues at every level for help (without seeming helpless) and show gratitude, plus real interest in what they do. For most people this signals you're on their side, and that's enough to win their active support.

Reach out

Kick-start your internal networking. Where are the people who can help you do your job well? Who can you learn from?

Don't rely just on your day one grand tour to meet new people. Seize opportunities to visit other departments or branches. Sit next to new colleagues every day at lunch. When introduced to new colleagues, don't just smile and nod – show interest in their problems and challenges, and be impressed by their successes.

Ask open questions about the way you can support what they do – and expect to hear some challenging replies. You may be the first person who has really listened to their needs for a while. However, ensure that you don't make too many promises at this stage because you probably have no idea how many you can deliver.

Spot career influencers

Some senior staff you encounter early are already making career-shaping decisions about you. You may already have met them at interview, in which case they formed (you can assume) a relatively positive opinion. However, other key decision-makers will be completely new to you. Think carefully about how you come across the first time you meet them. Looking flustered or confused, or sounding out of your depth, may tip them into thinking, 'I'm not sure this appointment was a good idea.'

Ultimately, of course, there will be key individuals who will decide about your future. This might not just be the person conducting your appraisal; it will almost certainly include your line manager, and your manager's manager. In a small organisation, your performance may be under scrutiny from the highest level from day one.

Think about first points of contact. You will be judged by the first time you touch every kind of task that comes up in your job: your first report, first meeting, first presentation. Probe the cycle of routine activities: don't be caught out by a sudden report deadline. Learn as much as you can about procedures and standards. Conformity may be uninspiring, but it keeps you out of trouble in your first few weeks. It also signals your ability to learn systems quickly.

Checking fit all over again

You performed a lot of decoding to get the job. Chapter 4 introduces you to additional ways of decoding your organisation as you arrive. This means doing something slightly odd – working out why you were hired.

Shouldn't that be obvious? You got the job, so surely you're a great fit – an exact match to the job specification? In practice, of course, you probably won't match every element in the job precisely; all appointment decisions are compromises. However, it is *very* useful to know which of your strong points made the organisation say 'yes'.

Seek this information carefully; it could sound like doubts about the job, or an insecure early request for positive strokes. Try a question like: 'Without this becoming an ego trip, I wonder if you could tell me what you saw in my background that seems most useful in this role.'

However you get this information, it helps you grasp working reality. It's a big, unambiguous signal of what an employer expects from you. You're not looking for point-by-point praise of how well you did at interview, but for a friendly discussion that highlights the things about you which the organisation sees as useful. This helps you understand what success looks like.

Ask for details about the way your performance will be assessed, both in the short term and further down the line. Seek insights into the kind of results which have marked out top performers recently. When your manager reviews your appointment in six months' time, what benchmarks will indicate success? What's the difference between 'good' and 'outstanding'?

Your questions about these performance criteria must not show any hint of insecurity, but should have an adult-to-adult flavour, along the lines of 'tell me what works for you'. Be clear about what information and evidence you will need to bring to your first review, so you don't face unpleasant surprises down the line (see Chapter 12 on appraisals).

From past to present

On day one, your world is brand new, but the team you join has a past. As you explore, discover your team's wins, losses, and near-misses – and find out what caused these varying outcomes.

Enquire sensitively about the person who held the job before you. Don't get drawn into any kind of negative criticism, you don't want to be seen as someone who has to trash someone else's reputation in order to build your own. Try to discover how long the previous post holder was in the role, highs and lows experienced, and why the person moved on. If you hear that past post holders experienced frustrations, see if you can overcome them using a different approach.

This book rehearses the way any of us can be 'set up to fail' (see Chapter 11). The phrase is widely used, often in reference to the first few months in a role. However, individuals sometimes tip themselves into failure – creating huge problems as they start in a new team, sending out all the wrong kinds of signals. They blunder into situations with insufficient reflection. They criticise working methods without understanding that the people they're talking to may have designed the very systems they are trashing. They are still very much in self-promotion mode and therefore often reinforce the idea that they are likely to over-promise and under-deliver.

Up to day one you've been in sales mode, pushing for a buying decision. From day one onwards, you are in career mode. Some people see their first 100 days as being about selling themselves to the organisation, when in fact it's more appropriate – and effective – to ease yourself in while causing as little damage as possible.

'Must do' list

- ✓ Be conscious of the stress of taking on a new role and plan carefully to protect yourself.
- ✓ Switch out of job-seeker mode into new employee mode.
- ✓ Increase your awareness of your starting reputation. Confirm the positive, challenge the negative.
- ✓ Identify potential blockers, brokers, and enablers as well as career influencers.
- ✓ Apply the range of strategies set out in this book to manage a soft landing.

4

The organisation and you

'Facts from paper are not the same as facts from people.' **Harold Geneen (1984)**

This chapter helps you to:

- Decode your organisation better
- See the bigger picture, from your organisation's perspective
- Organise a fast track check-in
- Get under the skin of role objectives
- Look at big ticket items

Decoding

As you start your new role, pause to think about how you got it. In order to get an interview and present as a bankable candidate, you had to do a lot of decoding – to work out, under the surface of the job description, what the organisation was really looking for. You looked at long lists of competencies and skills, and you worked out which items mattered most. Now that decoding continues.

Decoding sounds sophisticated, but many of us do it instinctively. As you prepared for interview questions, perhaps you decided which parts of the job description had the biggest weighting – the employer's 'must have' items. You might have compared details to similar roles elsewhere. You probably asked yourself, 'what are they really after?'. If your research was good, you possibly tapped into the expertise of industry contacts and recruiters to ask the same question.

Why the need to decode? After all, employers are in the communications business, aren't they? Nearly every organisation has a budget for carefully crafting internal and external messages. Most organisations have extensive websites. So why is decoding necessary?

There are several reasons. Job descriptions are often out of date, written by a committee, or they reflect competing agendas. Job descriptions and person profiles may be experimental, ambitious, unrealistic, or a reaction to a past hiring mistake. Often organisations don't understand, or don't articulate, key success factors. Sometimes, particularly if it's a new role, senior staff haven't decided exactly what the job requires and will revise the role as attractive candidates come along.

You have the power to decode. As stated, you've done some of this already, particularly when you prepared for interview questions. You may, however, neglect this process in your first few weeks – because you feel daunted by the complexity and strangeness of all things new. In today's frenetic work culture, induction programmes are short, if they exist at all (see Chapter 2), and new staff are expected not just to hit the ground running but to outsprint people already on it. Often new hires talk about facing a 'steep learning curve' in their starting month (see Chapter 13). This can sound like a white-knuckle ride, but the metaphor is a positive one – you're climbing the hill, not hitting a brick wall at speed.

Check out cultures

At first, new staff are treated like curious strangers, and then the dominant culture starts to assert itself. You quickly learn whether you're in a hostile or supportive environment. Organisations have personalities, just like people: some are friendly and positive, welcoming strangers; others are more reluctant to allow newcomers to change the chemistry of the workplace, and decidedly less responsive to new thinking.

Checking out a culture isn't just about getting a flavour of the organisation as a whole. It's also about spotting influential personalities and the dominant mindset. It means working out the pace, tempo, style of working and values of the organisation.

Read the runes. Learn cultural codes quickly – be clear on actions or information which need to be recorded. Find out how decisions are normally made, and what tolerance there is for making them differently under pressure. As Chapter 3 outlined, don't get caught napping by neglecting to file a routine report on time. Bureaucracy may be uninspiring, but ignoring it can trip you up.

Organisations offer at least two cultures. One is the version they spend money projecting to the outside world. In the public domain, organisations like to be seen as great places to work. Explore the 'careers with us' page of your new employer. Notice the photographs of staff with smiling faces? Note also the statements about diversity, learning opportunities, closing the gender pay gap. This is the outward projection of values and corporate behaviours the employer wishes the outside world to notice – its *employer brand*.

It's important to realise, in a healthy and pragmatic way, that employer brands are one picture of reality. This picture isn't necessarily a fiction: sometimes it's a fairly accurate representation of a positive environment where people enjoy their jobs; sometimes it's an almost complete inversion of reality. The problem is that all organisations say pretty much the same things. They say they're a great place to work, that they are reducing their impact on the environment, they invest in their people, and value their customers, stakeholders, the community, and the environment. Some fulfil promises, others fail on every count. It's difficult to tell from the outside whether you are looking at an organisation portraying itself honestly, or a well-polished piece of corporate spin.

Hidden cultures

On an everyday basis, employer branding boils down to a set of messages – the things an employer wants to communicate to potential new hires. The hope is that talent will be motivated to apply for jobs, and existing employees will recommend the workplace to others. The actual working culture may be very different to the one represented. This is the hidden culture, well known to current and former staff, often invisible to outsiders.

Your ability to 'read' this hidden culture can make the difference between walking tall and constantly looking at job vacancies. Most candidates know too little about working cultures before they take a job. Many people review the employer's website and accept everything that's been said at interview. Now imagine a worst-case scenario two months into the role, where those promises feel like claims from a second-hand car salesman. You discover what's going on behind closed doors: high staff turnover, power play, and unhappy staff.

Don't simply accept bland employer statements about a positive culture and engaged workforce – find out for yourself, ideally before you sign. Interviewers are part of the corporate PR machine, so asking 'what's it really like to work here?' will only result in positive-sounding noise (see Chapter 1). Talk to people who know the reality of working for the organisation (past and present employees, contractors and consultants); find someone who can give you bias-free feedback.

Even if you're already in a role, it's not too late to perform a cultural temperature check – it helps you to anticipate difficult problems and people (see Chapter 8). Share your initial impression with someone you trust. What's surprised and amazed you? What feels different? Dig deeper – what feels like a culture shock?

Looking for the bigger picture

Too many careers founder because staff don't have a big enough picture of the work they do. Their focus is on their immediate context; one job in one team. A failure to extend your job horizon is an indication that you've settled into a role, stopped decoding, and lost perspective (probably a career-limiting action – see Chapter 11).

The key questions here are about past, present, and future. What past needs led to your role being available? What does your job contribute right now, in today's climate? What value is your job likely to add two years from now? Failure to address these questions will make the difference between this role adding unremarkable evidence to your CV and career enhancement. How do you find the answers to these questions? Explore and learn.

Decoding requires investigation, comparing data from different sources, and making smart connections. Fortunately, looking like someone keen to learn everything new about a new organisation is one of the signs that the enthusiasm you brought to interview is going to be demonstrated on the job.

Initial investigation

Keep asking 'smart' questions – the kind of questions you might have pitched on your interview day as you were being shown round the organisation. That doesn't mean you ask questions about everything. Glib ignorance is a dangerous position statement. Your new colleagues are curious enough about you to answer a few questions, but will be worried or irritated if you ask things that would be revealed by a simple Google search. Look at what your organisation is saying to the media – this can often provide more information about where your job fits in than a month of induction meetings. Cross-check internal messages with what you hear elsewhere in the sector.

All this enables you to see your new organisation with enough perspective to understand the things that drive it (opportunities, growth, weak competition) and the things you might see as road blocks (limited technology, industry contraction, external competition, internal friction, organisational politics).

Find out quickly how much or how little to put in writing when confirming and recording decisions. Each organisation has its own informal rules on this. Sometimes a verbal commitment is enough, and at other times all decisions need to be documented. Stepping too far one way or the other can signal your lack of fit. Learn what is acceptable and necessary, and always do it with a light touch rather than sounding prim. If you can't get the tone right in an email, pick up the phone.

Fast track check-in

Soon after beginning the role, ask for some time with your manager. Much of the conversation will follow predictable lines: 'welcome aboard' and 'come to me if you need anything'. Sometimes you'll be asked for initial impressions, code for 'what have you learned?'. See the above comments on ignorance and helplessness.

This conversation is useful for one important reason: gaining more information about goals. You know what they are on paper, but what do they mean in practice? This is a good time to revisit objectives and outcomes (your acceptance of the job offer may be taken as your absolute, unthinking 'yes' to everything in the job description).

Interrogating expectations in your first month is useful, but needs a light touch. It can sound like you are renegotiating the job offer inappropriately. It can sound like apprehension or confusion. However, what you can do is to seek more information about the outcomes that really matter to the other person in this conversation (which may differ from broader goals – recognising the difference matters). Ask questions which clarify those outcomes or make them more concrete. Ask, too, about the resources available to help you achieve them (training, colleagues, information, technology). Saying an uninformed 'yes' may mean accepting failure before you begin.

Accept tasks, clarify goals, and then agree a point for an early progress report. Rolling your sleeves up and getting on with things sends the right messages, but there is a danger of wasted effort and early mistakes if you don't check in to ensure you're on the right track. An early progress review communicates proficiency and energy, and also allows you to negotiate your way round unpredicted barriers. However, this is *not* your excuse to come back in three weeks to say you haven't made any progress or still don't understand the brief.

Learn the local language

We have established that organisations use codes, often unwritten cultural codes. Talking about what you need or what you want to achieve means speaking in the right language. Managers often criticise subordinates for 'not getting it' or not being 'on the right page' – employer and individual seem to be speaking different languages.

Learn the language that key people in your organisation use. What metaphors dominate? Whether your company is into 'road maps' or 'cutting-edge thinking' or 'empowerment', it often helps to begin to match your language with the kind of language used by key players. Becoming more in tune with your organisation is like learning the nuances of regional dialect. You start to sound more like a local and less like a tourist.

Gaining traction

Research your employer as if it were a major new sales account you were trying to win. If you wanted to win a big contract, your research would be thorough: key people at the top and their backgrounds, the organisation's main themes and targets, and a list of recent achievements and future projects. How many of us really undertake that kind of basic research with our own organisation? We adopt a passive approach – 'I'll be told everything I need to know' – rather than hunting down data that can show us with great clarity where to make our contribution.

Your job description will list duties and responsibilities, and may say something about key performance indicators – or some similarly robust language that tries to measure role impact. If you work in a profit-oriented environment, it's usually clear how your job is benchmarked: sales turnover, profitability, time or money saved, business leads obtained and built upon. Some outcomes are more qualitative: customer satisfaction, for example, or staff retention.

Many job descriptions use vague terms like 'contribute to . . .' and 'assist with . . .'. Some employers, particularly those in the public and third sectors, include a mix of 'soft' (often subjective) and 'hard' (clear, measurable, and unambiguous) outcomes. The first group is more difficult to handle. If you are supposed to 'liaise with' or 'ensure effective communication', how do you know when you have succeeded? Organisations feel under pressure to list role objectives, but then write them in such a way that no one is clear how they are measured.

Probe the goals and targets you've been given. What do they actually mean? How do others interpret them? Seek information about how results are benchmarked, paying close attention to the results and behaviours which cause someone to be described as 'just managing', or 'average'. What kinds of outcomes are seen as noteworthy achievements? What makes someone's performance 'exceptional'? Delve deep into the organisational culture to find out what the language used to describe success means in practice. Look for concrete examples of completed projects and outcomes deemed as 'wins' (see Chapter 6).

As you negotiate a new role, use the **Job Focus Questions** below in discussions with colleagues and your line manager. You might not use the questions exactly as they are written – find your own, natural, wording.

Job Focus Questions

1. *What is the purpose of the job?* Why is this job being filled right now? What headache, problem or opportunity does it address?

2. *What does the job contribute?* What leverage does this job exert? What problems would arise if this job didn't exist?

3. *How does the job fit into the organisation?* How does the role depend on, or impact upon, others? How closely do role objectives match what the organisation wants to achieve?

4. ***What specific knowledge or skills are required?*** What else do I need to learn to be successful? How do I sharpen up my skills and knowledge?

5. ***What are the main problems to be solved?*** What can go wrong? What skills will I need to fix problems? How did previous post holders solve the same problems?

6. ***How much freedom is there to act or make decisions?*** What independence will I have in the post to use initiative or to implement change?

7. ***What controls or limits apply to the job?*** What are the budgetary, organisational or time constraints? What gets in the way of success?

8. ***What quick wins are expected and possible?*** What results need to be achieved quickly – and why haven't these problems been solved before? (See Chapter 6.)

9. ***What longer-term results does the job exist to achieve?*** What outcomes matter, and which outcomes are actually monitored? How is performance measured? Who will judge what is meant by success?

10. ***Who needs to be influenced?*** Who will support my efforts, and who will get in the way? Who do I need to inform and impress?

There are, therefore, many ways of decoding a job. It pays to establish an early reputation for delivery, while communicating clearly where anything significant blocks progress. What often matters is showing determination in the face of difficult circumstances, adding value in a way that surprises even your strongest allies, and demonstrating integrity in the face of unpleasant organisational politics (see Chapter 8). As you learn, talk about your discoveries as well as your ideas – showing and sharing a sound knowledge base.

Fully understanding the role and organisation are obviously key. Discovering how your organisation thinks is also vital. Getting ahead in your new role means acquiring great judgement about where to expend energy. In other words, *working hard on things that matter*. Using this chapter and the one that follows, work out the main focus of your organisation. Longer term, think about moving closer to a team that is more closely aligned to this agenda.

Look at big ticket items

Your first hours and days in the job are about spotting opportunities and challenges. Begin with information that is readily available to you about the strengths and weaknesses of your organisation. Either alone, or with your new team, look at the big ticket items:

Big ticket items	
What does the organisation do well?	What gets in the way of doing well?
What is the organisation known for?	What will change this reputation?

This builds on other models which look at an organisation's strengths, weaknesses, opportunities, and threats. Here's a more developed version:

Big ticket items unpacked	
What do we do well? (*How do we know?*)	What gets in the way of doing well? (*What are the external and internal barriers to success? What happens if nothing changes?*)

What are we known for? (*What do customers, competitors, industry contacts, existing staff, and potential hires say about us?*)	What will change this reputation? (*Change we have some control over, and change outside of our control*)

Understanding 'what we do well' means looking at brands, technological advantage, quality, knowledge and expertise, and market position. Problems arise where these advantages are vulnerable to change – people leave, and know-how becomes stale or out of date. An organisation can be very smug about its strengths, so a revealing (and disturbing) question is: 'What is the weakness inside that strength?' For example, a company's greatest strength may be the features of its top-selling product. How quickly and easily can those features be imitated by competitors? How long can you maintain your position in the marketplace? Barriers can arise from a wide range of factors, from bureaucratic obstacles, to poor resourcing, to a silo mentality.

The above grid looks at internal and external factors, and also looks at future possibilities. What opportunities have already presented themselves that you have yet to exploit? What threats can you perceive? This exercise works well on a small-scale level because you can act on results. You may be concerned about what you do when you discover negatives, but you may make a big impact by spotting early warning signals. The big ticket analysis above is great for generating great questions, and possibly some quick wins.

Your personal big ticket items

There is an analogy here with your own career position. You may take the positives in your situation too much for granted. If you have a great relationship with a key manager, what happens if that manager moves on? If your strength is your technical ability, what happens if a consultant offers your company an even higher skill level? If your strength is your knowledge, is it up to date? Big ticket analysis applied to an individual:

Big ticket items in your career	
What do you do well? (*How do you know?*)	What gets in the way of doing well? (*What are the external and internal barriers to success. What happens if nothing changes?*)
What are you known for? (*What could change your reputation?*)	How is your career going to change? (*What changes will you initiate, and what might be imposed on you?*)

'Must do' list

✓ Learn the art of decoding your organisation.

✓ Check out the real culture you're working in – not the one projected by the organisation in its employer brand.

✓ As you look at your new role, extend your horizon so you get the biggest possible picture of where your job fits.

✓ Ask intelligent, well-researched questions; avoid any impression of ignorance.

✓ Use the Job Focus Questions set out in this chapter to explore the background to your role and predict success criteria.

✓ Use the big ticket approach to explore where your organisation may be going in the future.

✓ Spend time learning the local language so you sound like a committed insider rather than a curious stranger.

Mapping the organisation

'Research is formalized curiosity. It is poking and prying with a purpose.' **Zora Neale Hurston (1942)**

This chapter helps you to:

- Learn how to map your organisation
- Identify gaps in your understanding
- Identify who can help you to fill in these gaps in knowledge
- Anticipate barriers to discovering information
- Spot information that will help you integrate into the new organisation
- Commit to an action plan for exploration and relationship building

Drawing better maps

Doing well in an organisation involves a dual process of insight and application – in other words, actively matching your career drivers (see Chapter 13) with the needs of the organisation. Your 100-day plan and beyond should be all about improving the quality and quantity of things you know about your present employer.

The checklists that follow will help you create a 'map' of your organisation. You will identify key pieces of information, and diagnose gaps in your knowledge, so you understand the basic homework you need to undertake to get on top of the job. Building on things you learned before interview, you will discover critical areas of knowledge that will have a major impact on your role. The organisational mapping process helps you develop a short list of the things you need to discover quickly. It's designed to encourage you to track down people you need to speak to, and commit to an action plan for shaping your future.

Mapping the organisation – guide to the tool

Why, when, how

Building organisational maps isn't really about drawing maps or charts or filling in a grid. It's about investigation through relationship building. This activity is definitely useful when you start a new role, but you can use it at other times too, such as when your role changes, your manager changes, or your organisation restructures.

This tool is something to keep to yourself – not one to share with your line manager or new colleagues until you know them well. If you were putting it in front of new colleagues, you'd be massaging results to improve your image rather than being honest about your areas for exploration and development. So, a tool for you to use alone – but one you might share with an external coach or independent mentor.

When do you use it? As soon as you've decided to accept the role. Even at that stage some gaps will be evident (product range, linked organisations, the names of key people). Others will become much clearer once you've started the role. The questions posed by this document provide great door openers – several good reasons to reach out to new people in the new organisation.

Checklist: Map 1 – The organisation

Key issue	Awareness score 0 = Zero 5 = Acceptable 10 = Extensive	Next action/next person I need to speak to improve this score	Barriers to discovery	When I will do this by
History of the organisation				
Market profile – size, profitability, market share, brand awareness				
Product range – what is your employer's best/worst selling product or service?				
What is your employer's most/least profitable/successful activity?				
What major new products or services are likely to come on stream in the next 12 months?				
What new products or services from competitors are likely to impact on your employer?				
Who is your employer's biggest customer?				
Who is your employer's biggest competitor?				

What differentiates your employer from your closest competitors?							
What's the media/public image of your organisation?							
What new legislation is coming along which may affect your employer or your job?							
What is your employer's track record for staff retention, recruitment, and training?							
Senior staff who connect to your role							
Who is likely to be promoted to a key position within the next 2 years?							
Who is likely to retire within the next 2 years?							
Who makes most of the decisions about staff development and training in your organisation?							
Other							

Checklist: Map 2 – How your role fits into the organisation

Key issue	Awareness score 0 = Zero 5 = Acceptable 10 = Extensive	Next action/next person I need to speak to improve this score	Barriers to discovery	When I will do this by
Who else in your organisation performs a similar role to you in a different department or division?				
What competencies are listed by your employer in connection with top performers?				
Your career prospects within your current department				
Prospects in a different department				
Cross-divisional opportunities you could participate in				
Colleagues at your current level with a different perspective on the organisation				

Colleagues at a higher level with a different perspective on the organisation								
Key specialist functions/communities that will impact on your future								
Identifying a mentor								
Identifying a coach								
Personal development, training, and coaching opportunities								
How you might fit into your organisation's talent management programme								
How key decision-makers see your contribution to the organisation								
How influential colleagues see your contribution to the organisation								
Other								

Column 1 topics

The topics provided here offer a generalised mapping technique. Some will work for your context, others will need to be adapted to the specifics of your role and organisation. Often the language will need to change. That's often your first discovery – what things are called.

Awareness score

In most areas of these grids, you won't give yourself a score of zero (unless you entirely bluffed your way at interview). Don't worry about making fine distinctions between one score and another, or avoid a score of 10 because it implies perfection. The point of scoring is to provide you with a reason to make progress, and to offer a direction of travel and reveal the things you need to do urgently. The scoring system rewards you for work undertaken, and shows you where you need to do more.

Next action/next person I need to speak to improve this score

The next column turns a question into an action. Some things require a little desk research, but every question in the grid is best answered in a conversation – ideally a face-to-face one. This is not just because of the information you obtain, but because conversations improve your visibility and help you build relationships with people who might impact on your role and career prospects.

Barriers to discovery

The most common barrier to discovery is that you don't yet know who to ask. Exploring solutions is part of the process, and part of what makes this task enjoyable. Sometimes barriers arise because you're working in a part of the organisation or in a location where you are cut off from certain kinds of people and information. That's one where you need to find a work-around, for example by speaking to people on the phone or at an event.

When I will do this by

Why set deadlines? Simply because this is a work task, and one that matters. Who are the key people who know the answers to most of the above questions – people you need to speak to within the next month?

As you can see, the idea of organisational mapping is that you commit to a process of exploration. Having identified key gaps in your knowledge, you commit to exploratory conversations. The power of this map is that it is a work in progress document – *and* a way of tracking progress and success in making connections.

This chapter doesn't contain a 'Must Do' list, because the exercise above offers a clear set of tasks. We will explore ways you will build on this mapping process in the following chapters.

6

Quick wins and slow burns

'There is surely nothing quite so useless as doing with
great efficiency what should not be done at all.'
Peter Drucker (1963)

This chapter helps you to:

- Understand the dangers of pushing for results without learning how to fit in
- Spot the equal danger of sounding cautious about implementing change
- Learn the essentials of the new role fast
- Observe and emulate valued behaviours
- Seek opportunities to implement quick wins
- Develop strategies to go beyond your job description
- Explore slow burns and longer-term career development

The balancing act

When new appointees are asked 'what difference will you make in your first 100 days?', their answers often fall back on cliché: 'Naturally, I'd take time to get to know my colleagues and really understand the organisation before I start to make changes.' This carefully balanced pitch runs the risk of making you sound like a cautious plodder. This approach may sound sensible, but it's dull, predictable, and safe.

At a time when organisations are reinventing themselves on something like a three-year cycle, waiting for a senior hire to take months to learn about an organisation before kick-starting change is a recipe for frustration.

Yes, you will need to learn things before you can act, and you will have significant gaps in your knowledge when you start a job. However, when asked about your initial impact, you need to demonstrate an astute mix of appropriately skilled planning *and* an apparent willingness to get stuck in quickly – in other words, promising results without appearing arrogant or naive.

Your first strategy is to learn how the best people perform in your new organisation. Identify three kinds of workers: people who everyone agrees are doing a good job, people who seem to make things happen, and people seen as rising stars. Observe their behaviours. How do they manage to communicate a positive attitude, ask for help, persuade people to cooperate? Learn the style of working your organisation prefers. For example, the organisation may value careful consultation before action, or it may prefer crisp decision-making and getting things done without fuss.

Talk to your new colleagues, even those way below you in the pecking order. Focus on how things are discussed more than facts: this stage is as much about relationship building as gathering information. Put the agenda of your colleagues before your needs. Ask questions which show you take in information quickly, but also questions which respect past work and current projects (see Chapter 3 on early impact).

Your plan, therefore, is to be *both* consultative and decisive – checking in, learning quickly, and then introducing something new. Your first 100 days are a balancing act between checking in to find out where your role contributes (or irritates), and taking the opportunity to achieve early results.

Show you're a fast learner

One quality that is almost universally prized in today's fast-moving world is the ability to learn fast. Evidence this by the quality of your questions, your follow-up questions, and by your ability to put learning into practice quickly. Make your most common message 'yes, I've been learning about that' rather than 'I'm new here so I don't know . . .'.

Look back at your past to remember occasions when you had to learn something fast. What learning style worked best for you? Watching a video? Reading a handbook? Getting someone to explain it to you? Watching someone operate and then copying what you see? Learn fast by learning in the way that suits you best.

Don't over-emphasise gaps in your understanding or sound helpless. Pointing to gaps in your knowledge might suggest you're not ready for the role. There's a big difference between 'this is interesting' and 'this is all very complicated'. Spending too long saying you feel out of your depth sounds like you might have faked your way through the interview. Since modesty is a useful social convention, new staff often describe the task of understanding the organisation as daunting or scary, when all that's required is a respect for complexity and strong evidence that you're learning fast.

Quick wins

The art of initial impact is doing things that matter, quickly. Make sure you deliver on your interview promises. Sometimes this isn't easy – particularly as you discover unseen barriers.

Start with the commitments you made at interview. Your employer took you on because of promises you made, explicit or assumed. If you make no effort to honour them, you won't be many weeks into the job before your colleagues are wondering if you 'walk the talk'. Showing early commitment to delivery matters, but so does thinking carefully about what you hope to achieve.

Some things you will want to implement require a long lead time. You need to absorb information, understand people, get a feel for what is possible and what, typically, gets in the way of change. Sometimes you need to win friends, or prove your ability, before you are allowed to fly solo.

Other solutions are, however, relatively quick and painless, and – if you've done something like it before – can be highly effective in terms of getting fast results and getting you noticed. These are *quick wins*. They have several characteristics:

Quick Wins

1. You bring experience or expertise to bear quickly
2. The time scale is short
3. You produce a measurable result
4. The cost and risk are low
5. The outcome is noticed

Sometimes quick wins are described as 'low hanging fruit'; in other words, obvious problems that can be solved almost effortlessly – projects offering an excellent return on small time investment. Opportunities like this may be within your grasp, but there won't be many – if all problems were easy to solve, the organisation wouldn't need to hire you to fix them.

Quick wins should closely match the immediate, voiced needs of the organisation; a problem or opportunity passes under your nose, or you discover it through enquiry. You may already have a solution up your sleeve. It may even be the kind of strategy you've talked about at interview where you said 'here's an idea which might be useful'.

In other words, a quick win is a small project or fix with a simple flavour. It is *low on cost* and *high on imagination*. What is the biggest impact you can achieve in the shortest time, with the minimum of effort and resources?

Turning ideas into action

New hires, especially if they are in management roles, often try to impose a detailed programme of change. This takes time, and often meets resistance. Quick wins take very little time to implement and, if you picked them right, face almost zero resistance.

Be careful how you suggest new ideas – you may be trampling all over someone's pet project. Don't criticise the way things are done currently, but build on what you discover. Make ideas sound like suggestions rather than directives. Share methods you have used in the past, rather than telling people how things should be done.

How do you find targets for quick win solutions? Look around you. What gets in the way of success, or dampens productivity? What can be resolved obviously and cheaply? What blocks and snags might be eradicated fairly quickly? Ask productive people, 'What could we do better?' and, 'If you could change one thing about the way you work, what would it be?' Refer to the organisational mapping you have undertaken (Chapter 5) and the data you've gathered. Do any common problems jump out at you which could be readily tackled?

Decide, or seek permission, to implement one or two changes which you deem low cost. In this context, 'cost' includes psychological cost as well as financial outlay;

implementing a change which make someone look foolish or lazy, for example, will be very costly in terms of long-term relationships. Similarly, aim for low-risk ideas; asking an organisation to restructure a process extensively may put your reputation at risk if things go wrong.

Pitching your idea as a pilot scheme or feasibility study may make permission easier to obtain. Managers are often more likely to accept a mini-project rather than a huge and permanent change. Make it sound as if you're proposing a practical experiment, offering to come back with some interesting results and feedback. Of course, pilot schemes can easily become established routines without anyone raising an eyebrow.

Make sure people understand where and when improvements have been implemented, but give credit to anyone who helped you spot where a win was possible, or assisted you to achieve your goals. Avoid gaining the reputation of being a one-hit wonder; follow up your first quick win with others.

Catch the wave

No matter how dynamic you are, you can only commit a finite amount of energy to work. In fact, working longer and longer hours will only produce limited benefits, and ultimately will degrade your performance – and your well-being. If you really want to work smarter, not harder, put your energy into projects which make the biggest difference and have the greatest visibility.

As you start to become established, identify an area of work that is currently – or will be – a strategic focus for the organisation. This should point you towards a project that's bigger and more impactful than a quick win. To identify this, you need to be tuned in to the overriding needs of the organisation. This needs excellent understanding of the organisation (see Chapter 5) so you align your efforts to key strategic objectives.

There is an element of luck in 'catching the wave' – gaining the right competencies at the right moment. Luck is, however, only a small element – the rest is about decoding and matching. As you work on your career awareness (see Chapter 12), you're far more likely to see the right moment and bring your experience to bear on an important issue. Discover the major concerns, if not obsessions, of key decision-makers. Find ways of connecting and working with these key individuals, maybe by taking on work in their area or by consulting them as part of your role. Individuals like this are often the ones to start initiatives and they will naturally attract teams of like-minded individuals, sometimes regardless of organisational hierarchy.

Enhanced visibility

As you approach the end of the first three months in the role, you should have a couple of quick wins under your belt. Next you will be thinking about initiating at least one major project. By that point you should know enough about what the organisation needs and the way it works to have decided what to pitch, and why. You should also know enough about people and culture to enable you to win the right support and the necessary resources. Decoding these elements will no doubt be made easier if you work with a mentor (see Chapter 12).

Think about how the project you have in mind will contribute to your visibility. Your contribution needs to be effective, but also memorable. Try making your actions OBVIOUS (see below).

Remembering the OBVIOUS

Your actions should be:

Observable – others will be talking about what you have achieved
Benchmarked – the effects are measurable and connect to organisational goals
Visible – to key decision-makers
Individual – the fact that this is *your* personal contribution will be clearly identifiable
On Target – focused on what matters to the organisation
Understood – people see the obstacles you had to overcome
Special – you do something that clearly differentiates you from internal or external talent

Expand on your job description

Think of your job description as a starting point rather than a destination. How elastic is your job? How far are you boxed in by your job description? If you think your job can't be altered or expanded, is this a restriction in the job, the organisation, or your mindset? How could you add maximum value to your organisation by making the smallest changes to your job?

To grow beyond your job, you need to establish a network of support, information, and encouragement – and then build on it. Begin by asking for information as part of your initial learning cycle, and then ask more penetrating questions about key stages in the process, as well as key people.

Don't just talk to people in your own team or department, but take opportunities wherever possible to understand the perspective of colleagues in other parts of the organisation, particularly those who have some influence over change (Chapter 5 provides an organisation mapping tool to assist you). Occasionally, you will get the chance to talk to key customers and suppliers as well. Find out how your new role links with these internal and external stakeholders and how that may change.

Check objectives – from every angle

Most management courses tell you that to succeed you need to meet clear, documented objectives. This is a good place to start: defining what you mean by success helps you recognise when you have achieved it. Review any documented objectives or targets attached to your role. What do they mean in terms of tangible results? Find examples of other people whose track record offers examples of best practice.

Investigate objectives thoroughly before you put energy into achieving them. Objectives might be on a functional level (to check and process 20 funding applications every week) or may be linked to quality standards (achieving above-average customer satisfaction ratings). The best kinds of objectives are measurable (so you know when you've hit them), and are responsive to planning (you know what you must do to reach them). Better still, objectives should be related to the bigger picture – where your organisation is going. Think like an investor, not just like an employee. If your money was at stake, what changes would you itch to make? Which levers can you pull, and which of them gives the biggest results?

Clear objectives will also assist your motivation; workers who see how their roles add to the larger picture are often more content. We all know about setting SMART objectives (Specific, Measurable, Achievable, Realistic, and Time-bound), the rather dated textbook basics. Why are these not universally effective? Largely because few of us leap out of bed on a cold winter's morning to fulfil objectives that are simply specific, measurable, and so on. We also need objectives that are energising and rewarding. These are the ones that make work interesting.

Objectives and outcomes

You're already aware from Chapter 3 that impact is about image as much as delivered role content. Businesses are built around perceptions as much as hard facts.

By analogy, look at customer relationships. Most surveys reveal that the main reason a customer leaves a business isn't quality or price. Customers switch to alternative suppliers largely because they feel they aren't being looked after. They felt loved once, and don't feel it any more. Perceptions, impressions, feelings, all these have a strong bearing on loyalty. How we *feel* about an experience is often more powerful than what happened.

Thus, there seems to be a difference between objectives and outcomes. *Objectives* are set, recorded, measured against, reviewed. *Outcomes* are emotional – how you made someone feel, and their memory of that feeling.

Imagine you're in a restaurant and you're ordering a meal. An objective-driven approach would focus on measurable standards: how quickly were you seated? How long did you have to wait to order? Was your food served on time, at the right temperature? Compare this to the feeling you get when a waiter remembers what you ordered on your previous visit. You're more likely to recommend a restaurant that made you feel special than one that fed you well; in the right atmosphere, all food tastes better. Real outcomes are less about conformity to standards and more about experiences you want to repeat.

Customer loyalty to brands and services is therefore about feelings more than facts. The same might be true about your career. You may think that moving forward is all about measurable objectives – ticking all the right boxes at your appraisal. Your successes will be noted, but few of them set the world on fire. People tick objectives – but remember outcomes.

What are outcomes in career terms? You make an emotional impact. You help, you inform, you impress. You make someone feel good or make someone look good. For example, you give someone your full attention rather than just listening, or you go the extra mile to help. You volunteer information which makes someone else shine. You make the person who hired you look good by making an effective and interesting presentation.

Outcomes beat objectives – every time! A meeting will have objectives (getting through the agenda, allocating work, agreeing a rota), but it will also have important outcomes – for example, people get on slightly better with each other at the end of the meeting than they did at the beginning.

This works for relationships with your boss, too. If your boss needs to look good or feel reassured, then work towards that outcome. If your boss has a particular hobby horse (wants you to be in work before her in the morning, hates surprises, wants you to remember people's names, or prefers ideas in writing before a meeting), achieving those outcomes may be more powerful than anything else in your job description.

Work with the grain rather than against it. Sometimes the key to success is being able to think like your boss (or your boss's boss) thinks. This isn't simply about shared language and emotional intelligence, but about realising what your boss finds important – focusing on your boss's biggest headache, and solving the problem.

Build up your knowledge bank

One quick win is cheap and simple: share information. Passing on information or background material which makes someone more effective is a low cost but effective way of building relationships.

Your perceived knowledge is part of your reputation. Here again the word 'perceived' matters – not just what you know, but how that knowledge is seen. Your knowledge may be highly specialised – inch wide but mile deep – and you might trade on this as your career brand. Specialised knowledge works in some contexts, broad knowledgeability works in others. Applied learning is almost universally valued.

If your academic or work background is slightly unconventional, rather different to your colleagues, use that to your advantage. Turn a mixed background into a strength rather than a flaw or eccentricity. You may be able to make multi-disciplinary connections, offering insights that others will fail to see.

Your knowledge bank

- Topics on which colleagues have asked your advice
- Areas of research or analysis you have undertaken
- Topics you have written reports on for internal use
- Topics you have written articles on in external media
- Subjects you have trained others in, or spoken about at staff seminars
- Areas of knowledge to which only a few individuals have access

Extending your areas of knowledge

- Seek parallels from other industries or sectors
- Find out how others achieve success and ask for their tips on shortcuts and minefields
- Find out as much as you can about the work of others; become a fount of knowledge on who does what
- Keep a resource book to record useful contacts and articles
- Attend conferences and seminars, subscribe to online discussion groups – keep up to date with new ideas and approaches

---

Showcasing your areas of knowledge

- Ask to be given the chance to produce surveys of best practice, specialist techniques, or resources
- Seek opportunities to benchmark against other organisations and sectors
- Contribute to in-house or industry journals
- Build a reputation as an information broker – a great source of data and connections
- Offer talks and workshops to show how what you know can inform and help others

---

Slow burns

Quick wins are high-impact. Slow burns have a longer-term agenda. What are you going to start off now that you might complete in 12 or 18 months? These projects need more care, and more planning. Committing too early to something which takes large amounts of time for minimal returns is clearly a poor idea.

Long-term planning should include your personal development. Discover what's on offer in terms of learning, mentor programmes, and the possibility of a career conversation (see Chapter 12). With some solid wins under your belt, review the learning you need to take you forward, and the kind of training on offer. What kind of case do you need to present to gain funding approval? Look at what others have done recently.

Career progression – an even longer game

Plan for unconventional progress. New employees often assume that a career ladder is best scaled step by step, and that someone will give you a shove up to the next level if you sit tight and do a great job. Very few organisations operate around such a traditional model. You may need to make at least one lateral move. Look at rising stars in the organisation to work out the experiences that are considered vital.

In order to progress in a complex organisation, you will need more to rely on than your own wits. Chapter 12 outlines the value of mentors. You will also need ambassadors and champions – people who communicate your value in a variety of contexts.

As the role unfolds, keep one principle in mind. Success isn't just about *doing things right* – hitting targets and avoiding error. It's also about *doing the right things*. Look at yourself objectively – are you offering what the organisation wants?

Your first aim is to contribute to the most important parts of the organisational agenda. Your second aim is to ensure that key people notice.

'Must do' list

- ✓ Balance 'checking in' with getting early results.
- ✓ Focus your attention on the things you need to learn quickly in order to become competent.
- ✓ Spot and implement quick wins.
- ✓ Try a pilot scheme.
- ✓ Focus on the OBVIOUS.
- ✓ Make your contribution count by thinking about where you can exert leverage and improve your visibility.
- ✓ Think about slow-burn, longer-term projects, including your own personal development.

Managing key relationships

'Remember not only to say the right thing in the right place, but far more difficult still, to leave unsaid the wrong thing at the tempting moment.' **Benjamin Franklin**

This chapter helps you to.

- Start building positive relationships in your new role
- Ask rather than tell
- Focus on fitting in with your new team
- Get off to a good start with the boss
- Demonstrate enthusiasm and engagement
- Learn how to talk about yourself at the right time and in the right style

Make people your main focus

In a new role you will spin a lot of plates. You'll be thinking about your initial impact. You will focus on learning things quickly. You will want to get a grasp on the things you need to deliver first. At the same time, you will be decoding the job (see Chapter 4) to find out what really matters in the role. Finally, you'll do your best not to tread on too many toes and to build positive working relationships. These need your close attention. Something that starts on day one with a handshake and a hello may turn out to be one of the best episodes in your career, or may be the first chapter in a long saga of misinformation and personal criticism.

Chapter 8 will look at difficult working relationships and cultures. This chapter explores ways of building positive relationships in your new role.

Start as you hope to finish

When you exit an organisation you will, with luck and effort, leave behind a small number of friends and a larger number of warm working relationships. How do you establish equally valuable relationships in your new role?

Think about the way relationships form when people meet you for the first time. People may assume you will want to impose ideas and seek opportunities to talk about your previous roles, your skills, and your experience. As Chapter 3 outlines, first impressions have long-term value.

Put your focus on asking rather than telling – asking great questions rather than talking about yourself. Getting people to talk to you provides all kinds of clues about their roles, their working style, and quickly points you to brokers and blockers (see Chapter 3). Discovering the things that sometimes go wrong is also a great way of anticipating road bumps before you hit them at speed. The final reason for staying in questioning mode is that you pick up insider language – knowing how an organisation describes a top performance is as important as achieving it.

From settling in to fitting in

Becoming established in a job involves several stages. First of all there is the initial shock of arrival where you discover how little you know. Then you begin a process of induction, a stage that is about discovery and learning. Beyond that you're moving into something more like a period of transition where you learn the norms of the organisation and work out the best way to fit in. You will be applying skills and knowledge required in your past, but often through negotiation rather than imposing your views.

Senior managers will always compare new employees and the way they land. Many observe that new hires, if anything, try too hard to perform and don't put the same energy into fitting in. It's easy to see why. At interview you are asked what you will *do*, not how you will *be*. However, successful integration is very much about blending your personality with the group, gaining acceptance into a new tribe.

Much of what we know about the way teams form helps us understand what's going on here; a new member of a small group reshapes everything. You need to demonstrate credibility, gain respect, but also reassure. You need to look like an insider rather than a temporary visitor or external adviser.

For this reason, demonstrating the right attitudes is vital, and this will include a degree of humility – sounding like a well-informed learner. If this sounds a little like neglecting promises you made at interview to hit the ground running, you are partly correct. In the long term, adapting to a new environment and building effective relationships is going to be far more beneficial to your future career. In other words, you can't force your way into acquiring a new track record – you have to negotiate it as part of working in a team.

Joining a new team

Your first few hours of exposure in a new team are not just a chemistry check, but the beginnings of a vital relationship. Be aware that the team will check in later the same day and initial conclusions will be drawn about whether you fit in.

The most powerful way to ensure positive feedback is to put your attention on the team rather than on yourself. Signal your willingness to listen, and your curiosity to find out about best practice.

Pay attention to all members of the team, not just the team leader or the people with the strongest personalities. Getting alongside people early in the process can open all kinds of doors, and provide access to very useful information.

The ability to work collaboratively and consultatively in teams is highly valued. Strong team players can point to evidence of working in teams where there was friction, or unclear goals. Look at your experience. What role do you naturally adopt in a team? Do you lead from the front or organise the back room stuff? Do you progress, chase, cajole, persuade, encourage? Do you generate new ideas or build on other people's thinking? Do you ensure good communication, making sure people get on with each other as well as with the task? Remember that the work done to hold teams together is often about soft skills: open communication, collaborative working, sharing glory and blame alike.

The greater your awareness of your natural team contribution, the greater the chance you will settle into a new team easily. One obvious sticking point is where someone in the team is already filling the role you would naturally occupy. In these circumstances, adapt to fit into another role where you can add value. Effective team members know which roles they occupy comfortably, but also how to switch hats when required.

Avoid drawing from the past

You might arrive in your new organisation as an outsider, with a different background to most of your colleagues. As Chapter 3 outlines, their expectation is that you will quickly be saying, 'this isn't how we did things when I worked for X'. Since others may expect you to say you've seen it all before and done things better elsewhere, ensure the caricature doesn't fit.

Win people over

Relationships probably matter more than anything else in your new role. Open relationships mean people naturally feed you with useful information and make your life easier. However, those relationships are not built entirely from work interactions; often the key is genuine conversation.

Working harder and smarter than anybody else will have almost no impact on building relationships, which are built through social interaction. Take an interest in other people. Listen attentively, giving people your full attention. Adopt the politician's trick by making your conversation partner feel like the most important person in the room for 60 seconds. As Chapter 3 outlines, starting a relationship in the right way can have impressively long-term benefits. So, when you ask, make it clear that you are listening, and then be clear to thank someone for their help.

Chapter 1 introduced you to the idea of due diligence. Time spent understanding the people around you is equally powerful. New hires who do well take time to understand how their new colleagues see the world, the things they value, and the things they find frustrating or irritating. Take time to interact with the wide variety of people in your new organisation, respecting the wide range of working styles you encounter.

When talking about social interaction, this can of course mean pretty much any kind of conversation, including small talk. There's no particular reason to confine yourself to work-related topics, unless that's all your colleague wants to talk about. If someone remembers you warmly because you share their taste in music, excellent. Showing respect for people means appreciating them in their entirety, rather than just focusing on the work they do.

Understanding role content better

There will inevitably be part of your role you don't fully understand. Since job descriptions are imperfect documents, don't be too surprised to discover inaccuracies. You may also discover that the emphasis of the job is rather different to what you expected; in other words, job documentation didn't explain what you'll be doing most the time, and what really matters.

Before asking for clarification, ask yourself a key question: 'Does it matter?' If there is a mismatch between your job description and reality, one of the best ways of dealing with it is often to just take it in your stride. Going back repeatedly to ask for clarification or for an explanation of apparent contradictions is a fairly negative signal. In your mind you are trying to do the job better, but an employer often hears disappointment; it sounds as if the job isn't what you had hoped for.

We've outlined the ways you need to adapt to a new role, and adapting generally means compromise. You should expect to hear slightly differing views about the requirements of your job, and you should certainly expect something of a reality gap.

If the gap is important, for example you expected to take responsibility for a project but you discover that someone else has been given the task instead, then raise the matter appropriately. In the same way that you maintained a positive tone when negotiating a job offer, keep things upbeat. Minimise the effect the issue has on you. Rather than saying

'I've hit a big problem', begin a conversation 'can I talk something through with you?'.

Be very clear about any tasks allocated to you – scope them out properly. Some of this will be in your own time, but it generally impresses to be able to summarise the key outcomes back to the person who is delegating the job in your direction. Negotiating time for the task is also a useful skill set, and so is setting review points. Learn to do this with a light touch: 'Can I give you a progress report early next week and let you know if I hit any snags?'

Next look at the resources you need to get the job done – tell people what you need. This could be about people, or information, or access to learning. You may also need support in terms of the way you're managed. As you get to know people better, you can be explicit if you know you work better when you receive honest feedback and more than a little encouragement.

Getting on with your boss

Work out your boss's thinking style. Is your boss focused on detail, or the big picture? Is your boss naturally democratic, consultative, or autocratic? Learn how your boss prefers to receive new information and questions. Don't double-check every detail; learn where you can act on your own initiative and where you need to seek authorisation. As you gain experience, you may find that seeking forgiveness after a decision offers more freedom of action than always obtaining prior approval – but that means you have to know your superior well.

Use contact time with your boss effectively. Frequently popping in for a 'quick word' distracts, and reinforces the idea that you have problems working unsupervised. Plan discussions carefully, using an informal verbal agenda ('I'd like to talk to you about three things – have you got a couple of minutes?'). Keep your boss informed (but not over-informed); communicate in a concise weekly report. Use a 20/2 approach: a short written briefing that takes you 20 minutes to compose, and your boss two minutes to read.

Learn the art of managing upwards. This might sound manipulative, or a means of attempting to pass work back to your boss. In fact, the practice means transparency about who does what, and when – and achieving this clarity with a light touch. If you really do have to hand a task back untouched, have a very good reason for doing so.

As well as considering the tasks you perform, think about emotional impact. People remember feelings far longer than facts. For example, making your boss look good, snatching victory from the jaws of defeat, winning back an unhappy client, these become core narratives that can shape your future. Making sure your boss feels warmly about what you do is the most effective way of managing this key relationship.

Appropriate influencing

Many stages of your career require highly developed interpersonal skills, especially the ability to communicate, influence, and negotiate. This chapter explores how you use these skills without falling into the classic trap of treading on toes by implementing ideas too quickly.

Although this book focuses on your first three months in a role, the whole of your first year is important. By the end of that year, you will most certainly have lodged a reputation in the minds of key players. You should also, within 12 months, have amassed useful evidence with which to populate your CV.

Parts of this book have looked at ways of managing your reputation. You might think this is a shorthand code for self-promotion. We've established that working hard does little to ensure success, and sometimes even achieving all your role objectives is not enough. You recognise that the key step isn't effort, but applying effort to the things that really matter to an organisation. There is still a further step: people have to notice.

The mistake we often make is to assume that the only way to draw attention to ourselves is self-promotion. Indeed, there is a lot of evidence pointing to the way we have turned assertive self-aggrandising into the new norm. Susan Cain's book *Quiet* (2013) outlines the way Business Schools in the USA reward extrovert and dominant behaviours in discussion groups.

In a similar way, we have allowed ourselves to believe that the only way to achieve career success is to adopt a mindset where you become the loudest voice in the room, impose your personality on others, and influence assertively until you get the results you're looking for. This is widely recognised as 'alpha-male' behaviour, although is not of course exclusively exhibited by men.

I don't feel comfortable pushing myself forward

It's perfectly reasonable to have doubts about self-promotion. Saying 'I'm the best thing since sliced bread' gets the attention of an audience, but it's important not to believe all your own PR.

There are other ways of achieving success than being an ultra-confident, high-energy performer. When it comes to ascending the career ladder, it's easy to assume that the only way to operate is to receive some kind of personality transplant. For quieter people, this is never going to work. Reflective introverts can choose to operate on the very edge of their comfort zone, especially when they are in 'performance' mode (for example, when presenting to an audience). However, their natural working style is to reflect carefully before acting, and to influence through relationship building rather than more direct behaviours.

Another great misunderstanding in modern working culture is that successful leaders are all loud self-promoters. You only have to meet a relatively small sample of senior executives to know that this isn't the case. Confident introverts are capable of communicating their views in a timely and forceful fashion when necessary, but are also very good at building deep relationships of trust.

However, this doesn't let quieter people off the hook. Self-promotion is a form of narcissism, but there are many times when we do need to project an image of ourselves in such a way that other people notice our presence and contribution.

Communicate energy rather than ego

This book looks extensively at the way an organisation reads its new hires, suggesting that attitude and personality play a big part. *How* you do things matters as much as *what* you do.

Energy matters in communication. We communicate energy in many different ways. A great deal is through body language, and that can be hard to rehearse or put on as a performance. However, the words we use and the stories we tell also contain energy. When you respond to a new idea with words such as 'exciting', 'inspiring', 'creative', you bring energy into the room, and demonstrate enthusiasm. Enthusiasm is identified as a key indicator of engagement, being on board, being connected to the organisation. Even if your natural style is to be contained, use high-energy words anyway. If you're given a new task, show interest in it, and choose language which signals enthusiasm. Being considered reserved or detached is another way of someone doubting whether you really fit in.

We've established that you are going to hold back on discussing your ideas and experience. Even so, people will sometimes ask direct questions about your background. Offer a short, factual summary, unembellished by adjectives – this is not a moment to sell yourself. There is one exception to this – when questioned by a senior manager who seems to be probing to find out if hiring you was a good idea. When someone like this asks, 'what ideas have you got for us?', that's a moment to bring something practical into the conversation and not a time for undue modesty.

Get used to talking about yourself; be concise, clear, interesting, and memorable. Practise talking about yourself in a style you find comfortable. Focus more on the content, the facts, if you prefer, rather than on your own actions. When it comes to your first appraisal (see Chapter 12), find a style of communicating your strengths that works for you – a style that gets you remembered, but doesn't make you feel like a fake.

Take the focus off yourself

Seek conversations, not speech-making opportunities. Show genuine interest in other people's experience and responses, and when you talk about yourself, remember that people want to be engaged in conversation, not broadcast at. Even when someone asks about you, focus on your areas of interest more than your skills. Talk about ideas, products, brands, technologies you find fascinating, and areas of research you've found stimulating. 'I'm fascinated by . . .' is much easier for a listener to hear than 'My strengths are . . .', and it opens up the conversation more securely.

The art of marketing provides useful parallels. Marketing isn't obsessed with the qualities of a product, but focuses on the needs of the end user. It focuses on a question ('what do you need?') rather than a statement ('this is what I am selling'). Empty self-promotion is like unfocused selling – pushing something the hearer doesn't need or want.

Self-marketers spend more time listening than talking. They discover. They listen to what people need. They pick up the right language, and become sensitive to the concerns and hopes of the organisation. Most of all, they look for the big picture. Whether your forte is managing the details or kick-starting the next project, always try to have a sense of how this contributes to the organisation in the widest sense – and if you don't know, find out.

A word of warning: be aware that there will be others around who are true self-promoters. Sometimes the worst kind of self-promotion works, even when it's driven by vanity, narcissism, and a Machiavellian lust for power. The worst kind of sales techniques (pushy, insensitive, manipulative) work up to a point. It's equally true that fraud, deception, and mugging old ladies can create an income stream. These methods get results, but often not in the long term, and always at a cost: to the person behaving this way, and to those on the receiving end. It's all too easy to acquiesce to this kind of behaviour, or – worse still – believe that this is the only behaviour that will get you success in your organisation (see Chapter 8 on organisational politics).

Look at the full range of senior figures in business life, and you'll find that there are a wide range of personality types, and a wide range of personal values. You can find ethical and sensitive people at the highest levels (just as you can find mean-minded, bitter, and self-obsessed people at every level in an organisation). Three things, however, come out in most surveys of business leaders: they have the ability to deal with people, the ability to have a strong vision and work towards it, and they have sufficient personal strength to remain true to themselves through the ups and downs of the process.

If you are genuinely worried that the price to be paid for career advancement is unacceptable, you probably want to explore this further. Is it a genuine fear that you have negative characteristics that will be emphasised or exploited? If you have a tendency to cut corners or bend the truth, will you become really lazy or dishonest? Or is there something about the way you read the organisation that makes you believe you will have to behave in unacceptable ways?

'Must do' list

- ✓ Use first meetings with new colleagues to listen, learn, and ask great questions.
- ✓ Put more effort into fitting in than impressing.
- ✓ Take time to read your new team before working out what you will contribute to it.
- ✓ Find out how your boss likes to receive information and make decisions.
- ✓ Learn how to influence appropriately and authentically – without looking guilty of self-promotion.
- ✓ If you find it difficult to talk about your skills and background, practise.

8

Road blocks – difficult situations and people

'The great enemy of communication, we find, is the illusion of it. We have talked enough; but we have not listened.'
William H. Whyte (1950)

This chapter helps you to:

- Anticipate and handle pressure
- Plan for difficult conversations
- Communicate sensitively in delicate situations
- Manage people older and more experienced than you
- Deal with uncomfortable work cultures and strong personalities
- Cope with organisational politics and manipulative behaviours

Immediate high pressure

The pressure you are put under in the opening months of your job is largely predictable. With luck, you will have agreed clear objectives for the things you will cover. The biggest pressure, naturally, is learning enough about the job to look as if you're in control.

If you're under pressure in ways you didn't expect, work out why. Being thrown in at the deep end will induce anxiety, but this is normally a temporary phase. If the role is more demanding than you predicted in the longer term, that might mean that it is a slightly different role to the one you had in mind, or simply that you hadn't anticipated the pace of working. Alternatively, circumstances might have changed, or you could be dealing with an emergency. Therefore, it's very important to ask if the problems you're dealing with are routine, or out of the ordinary. Everyday problems have pre-set solutions; the unusual may require your ingenuity. High-profile, unpredicted problems almost certainly require an early meeting with your line manager. In the meantime, make a visible effort to adapt and keep positive under fire. Surviving in a time of crisis will do great things for your reputation.

If you're given a challenge at the outset which pushes you way outside your comfort zone, pause before taking this to your manager. Consider if you knew this was coming – or should have worked it out as part of your due diligence (see Chapter 1). Should you have anticipated this part of your role? If you do raise the issue, don't be unrealistic about resources. Nearly everyone would appreciate more help and more time. Equally, avoid appearing needy; work out a way of resolving the problem without creating a negative impression.

Saying 'no' without closing doors

Before we say more about saying 'no', remember that saying 'yes' is generally preferable in a new role – unless you're saying 'yes' to something so outside your skill range that you may mess it up, or something that gets in the way of other vital projects. Saying 'yes' to everything, or all the wrong things, is clearly a way of cluttering your job up so much you will never focus on things that make difference. Saying 'yes, but . . .' occasionally can help you avoid being seen as a doormat – an unthinking people pleaser.

On the other hand, being known as someone who usually says 'no' puts you in the category of 'difficult'. Learn how to say 'no' appropriately without damaging your reputation. Several kinds of 'no' come across as 'yes'. For example: 'I can see your problem', or 'I can't take that on right now but I'd be happy to talk it through with you', or 'I'd love to take this on, but I've got a deadline'.

You can only do this occasionally in the first few months. If you're swamped and under pressure to accept more work, establish priorities. Is the new task urgent, important, or both? What tasks will now be pushed off the bottom of your 'to do' list? Saying 'I can do this but I will have to drop project A for a while' will help, and can begin a longer-term rethink of your role.

Taking important new duties in your stride helps you to be seen as a 'go to' person. Once you've said 'yes' a few times, it's reasonable to push back on additional, low-value tasks.

Handling difficult conversations

One of the pressures you will inevitably face in a new role is where conversations go wrong. Sometimes this will be because you haven't yet eased yourself out of your former work culture. Sometimes it's because people are making life difficult. Chapter 3 identified brokers, blockers, and enablers; you will no doubt encounter a range of attitudes.

Some of the conversations you will have in your first few months will be easier than others. Your arrival, even the role you occupy, may be seen as threatening. Or you may be talking to someone whose natural style is to be combative.

If you have a difficult conversation coming up, stand in the other person's shoes. Don't think just about what you will say, but how it will be heard and its emotional impact. When you have said what you plan to say, how will the listener be feeling – both immediately and half an hour after? You will have seen managers who drop verbal bombshells into conversations and later sound surprised that someone is upset. Effective managers plan for both ends of the conversation. This requires emotional intelligence.

If you're unsure, there are two ways to anticipate the impact of what you will say. First, find someone with better people radar than you and ask, 'how is Dave likely to react to this?' Second, don't improvise. Take time to plan what you will say – exactly. Rehearse tone as well as content. The words to prepare with most care are the words you use to set up the meeting, the words you speak when the conversation starts, and what you say when you try to get the most difficult part of your message across. If your opening gambit is 'We have a problem', you start in conflict mode; in contrast, 'How do you feel the presentation went?' treads carefully. Avoid generalisations ('people are telling me . . .').

Walking in other people's shoes isn't just about difficult messages. Your actions shape the way you are seen, and if you're going to stay ahead of the curve it's good to check in occasionally to find out how you're seen by others. An astute mentor (see Chapter 12) will help.

Communicating with care

Avoid putting difficult messages in writing. Even a short email can cause long-term damage to a relationship. Under pressure, don't react electronically. Tone is not always easy in a text or email; once adrenalin kicks in, your sensitivity to nuance goes out of the window. If a relationship isn't working terribly well, a thoughtless email can tip it over the edge.

In difficult situations take time to think and talk things through with a trusted colleague before you take the conversation forward. In nearly every case it's better to pick up the phone than to send an email, and better still to talk to someone face to face.

Managing people older or more experienced than you

Tricky conversations can occur where you're required to supervise or manage staff who have been in the organisation a long time. This takes sensitivity and tact – but a clear message that you're in charge. Experienced workers are more likely to want to work in their own style, and may feel they can do the job better than you. Lead from the front by demonstrating the skills that got you the job. It helps if you say why you want things done a particular way, or explain some of the pressures on you, but firm clarity is vital.

Alternatively, you might be a younger person with good ideas working with an older manager who resists them; or a 'digital native' trying to demonstrate problem-solving to a 'late adopter' manager. Finding ways of doing this without undermining the manager's experience or making them feel insecure or threatened takes a great deal of tact.

Another problem arises where you're required to manage staff who are not only experienced but significantly older. For some this won't be a problem, but others may resent your presence, particularly if they wanted the role you occupy. Avoid falling into the stereotype of the over-promoted younger manager (bossy, naive, lacking real job knowledge) by listening, consulting, and learning from the experience of those around you. Find a light touch. 'It would be great if this was finished by Friday' gets different results to 'I want this by Friday.'

Make the most of someone's experience and expertise without being patronising. Insecure managers tell people what to do and how to do it. Secure managers tap into existing knowledge. Begin a conversation with 'I'd like to pick your brain' or 'I'd value your advice.' Be open to learning things from people who have been around for some time, but be clear who makes the final decision.

Remember that for some people being managed by someone younger might be a painful reminder that they have hit a career ceiling. Address the issue specifically: ask how your colleague feels about being managed by someone younger, and what you can do to make that easier.

Uncomfortable work cultures

In work, information can be a tool, or it can be a weapon. If you find yourself left out of the loop on important issues, it could be the result of a difficult work culture. This might feel like a kind of lethargy, or unwillingness to change. The culture might be highly competitive ('if I am to win, someone has to lose') or might be toxic (where staff are sabotaged, bullied, or subject to unprofessional behaviour).

As we discussed in Chapter 1, asking questions about work cultures during interviews rarely produces an accurate picture. Cultures may reveal themselves slowly. Colleagues tip-toe around you at first, and then behaviours or comments are tested on you to gauge your reaction – perhaps personal or cynical remarks, or inappropriate humour.

How you react can make a big difference. Do you show how keen you are to fit in, or do you set red lines for what you will tolerate? The answer to that question is about integrity, but it's also true that toxic work cultures maintain themselves because of complicity, and looking the other way. Today's work culture is highly attuned to inappropriate behaviours, and the bar is constantly being raised on what's acceptable – often for very good reasons.

If the culture is truly toxic, you'll know about it quickly because you'll be under pressure to conform or resist. You face a dilemma. Should you suppress your personality and ethics and keep silent? Few people are happy with such a compromise because it creates feelings of unease, sometimes even grubbiness. If there is a mark of a good job, it is that you take your authentic self to work, and people value you for what you are, not what you pretend to be.

In a difficult work culture, look at what you can change, and what you can't. Be clear whether it's just your local team that is dysfunctional or the wider organisation. A mentor (see Chapter 12) can sometimes answer your question, 'is it me?' A coach may help you work through a strategy for changing the things within your control.

If your plan is to stay in the organisation and, ideally, rise to a senior position, look hard at the culture you're buying into. Look at the aspects of culture you're resisting, and those you are reinforcing. Career progression shouldn't be about the damage you do to other people in order to get to the top. Shark-like behaviour sometimes works in the short term, but destroys trust and leaves you short of friends. Success should be about standing on the shoulders of giants, not clambering over others in a mad scramble to the top.

Take the long view. How many of the people who backstab their way to the top have long-term friendships in work? How many of them could go back to a past employer and ask for help?

Handling organisational politics

What do we mean by organisational 'politics'? The word 'politics' originally referred to the life of citizens and the cities they lived in; in other words, how people get on with each other in organised systems. The way human beings behave at work is no better and no worse than they behave in other settings. However, work has a bigger impact on your self-esteem than some other areas of life – being in a difficult work environment will have more of an effect on you than belonging to a dysfunctional tennis club.

People in organisations behave tribally. The positive aspects of being tribal are loyalty, mutual protection, and safety in numbers. The negative aspects are conflict within the tribe and with other tribes, a tendency to marginalise those who don't fit in, and sometimes a reluctance to change.

When people talk about 'politics' in the workplace, the phrase usually comes with a grimace. Often there is a history of mistrust or unproductive competitiveness. At other times, you may experience truly manipulative and destructive behaviours.

Many situations are irritatingly intangible: life is made uncomfortable for you but no one is overtly hostile. Vital information reaches you late, or not at all. Possibly you're being given what in military life is called 'all assistance short of actual help'. Your request may be ignored because you're associated with a team or a manager who is out of favour. Inter-departmental rivalry can often absorb far more energy than beating external competition.

Organisational politics rarely improve communications or sharpen performance. It's a game which loves winners and losers, and those on the wrong side of the deal can experience deception, manoeuvring, even an unhealthy interest in making sure others don't succeed. Politics at work often causes confusion, a failure to move towards shared objectives, and is a reason why talented workers move on.

Look back at any times in your career when you have been blocked by 'political' behaviours – or complied with them, perhaps with good motives. The cost of playing organisational politics is *loss*: loss of integrity, loss of meaningful relationships, sometimes even loss of self-belief. Very few people go into retirement wishing they had been more cunning at work.

How do you survive in a politicised environment, when you're supposed to take sides, toe the party line, say which side you're on . . .?

20 Steps to Getting Around Organisational Politics

1. *Be aware of the politicians.* That's more than being aware of your discomfort: you need to recognise the people who are the key influencers in the organisation.
2. *Look at the damage.* Identify what goes wrong as a result of playing politics – the deals that are missed, the talent that leaves the organisation. Discuss the downside with your colleagues.
3. *Watch your back.* Are you treading, inadvertently, on someone else's toes? Are you in somebody's way? Many honest, diligent people just don't see the knife coming in their back. Recruit or work alongside others who have better 'radar' than you.
4. *Draw your line in the sand.* Before the crunch comes, be clear about what you are not prepared to do to win.
5. *Be honest.* There really is no other policy, and you have to have a tremendous memory to tell lies in an organisation. But remember that being honest doesn't give you carte blanche to criticise others. See **Step 6**.
6. *Praise or be silent.* Remember your mother's advice: 'If you can't say anything nice, don't say anything at all.' Try to find something positive to say about your colleagues, or keep your peace.
7. *Avoid gossip.* Okay, it's fun, but be careful to spot the line between discreet observations and character assassination. Distance yourself from toxic attitudes and people.
8. *Find people you can trust.* There are even-handed, open, helpful people in every workplace. Encourage them by helping them, providing useful information, and showing you do a great job.
9. *Identify the politics-free zones.* There are usually some key managers or decision-makers in organisations who manage to bypass the cutting and thrusting. Get them on your side, and follow their strategies.

10. ***Check how far your success means someone else's failure.*** Getting ahead requires competition, but doesn't have to cause someone else's downfall.

11. ***Accentuate the positive.*** You may find yourself surrounded by negative comments and thinking. It sometimes takes only a small effort to encourage people to see the glass as half full rather than half empty.

12. ***Move out of cynical teams.*** Such teams achieve very little, because they start from the position that it's all been tried before and there's no point anyway. If you're in a team like this and Step 9 fails, try independent activity.

13. ***Seek common ground.*** Even where people are at loggerheads, it's usually possible to find an outcome that works for both parties.

14. ***Be consistent.*** It's no use having integrity one day and being a conniving manipulator the next.

15. ***Do what you say you will do.*** Try it; it gets results. Fail to deliver (without explanation) and everything you say becomes an empty promise.

16. ***Set time aside to help others.*** Consider this time well invested, and do it because you can, not because of any leverage it gives you.

17. ***Help your boss win.*** Make your boss look good – but not at the expense of making someone else look bad.

18. ***Keep integrity as your surprise card.*** You know what 'integrity' means to you. Stick to your principles, and don't dilute them. Being straight and honest may make you the organisation's greatest asset. The honest, non-manipulative strategy is often the one that surprises.

19. ***Lose gracefully.*** If others jump the queue, push you aside, or outmanoeuvre you, don't be tempted to play by the same rules. He who lives by the sword . . .

20. ***Consider moving on.*** Don't use your failure to handle the politics as a stick to beat yourself. Organisational politics are hard to manage, even for the best operators. If you can't find a way to handle it, can't find the right allies, and your personal integrity is threatened too often, it may be time to move out (see Chapter 13). And when you do, don't let your main message to your next employer be about the damage the organisation has done to you.

Self-promoters and divas

It's wise to acknowledge that some of your colleagues will be fully fledged self-promoters. They will use every trick: ego-massaging, manipulation, half-truths and lies. It's all too easy to believe this is the only behaviour that achieves success.

Strong egos are important to organisations. They get things done through strength of personality and high-level influencing skills. Difficulties arise when personalities tip into narcissism – when people fail to respond to criticism and seek only flattery.

More unstable egos are often described as office 'divas' – where exuberant performance requires high maintenance. Diva-like behaviours are expressions of childlike frustration where people are not receiving unadulterated praise, or things are just not going the way they would like. You can generally judge where strong personality tips into unhealthy egotism: look where an individual focuses attention. If it's on tasks, problems, or working with other people, that's effective. If an individual's attention is on his or her own feelings and self-importance, you have a problem.

If you find yourself working in the shadow of a powerful ego (especially if this is your line manager), look hard at the consequences. In theory, the self-awareness of such personalities can be adjusted by 360° feedback. Sometimes even this has no effect; in general, behaviours like this are fairly unlikely to change. Pure egotists can operate in a bubble, impervious to feedback. If they create havoc or tread on toes, they are unlikely to feel they are part of the problem.

Dealing with high-maintenance characters like this requires energy, and discernment – be clear about the difference between situations where you can influence change and make a difference, and those where you can't.

Work with the grain rather than against it – place yourself in contexts where you're valued rather than just tolerated. Try to locate yourself in teams where colleagues get the job done, cooperatively, and where toys stay firmly in the pram.

Being pushed into a corner

If someone is making your life hell at work, don't assume you have to grin and bear it. Every employee has the legal right to enjoy a workplace free from bullying, sexual harassment, and victimisation. If you're on the sharp end of these behaviours, take advice. However, 'unacceptable' behaviour often falls in a legal grey area, and formal procedures require long, hard, isolating battles.

Think about what looks like a good outcome for you. Are you looking for justice, compensation, or simply the opportunity to get on with your job in peace? Official procedures may redress the balance or get you bogged down in a long battle; sometimes it's better to move on.

Do be aware, however, of the serious impact on your overall reputation if you make any complaint, large or small, in your first 100 days. In a difficult situation, take informal advice first.

'Must do' list

Dealing with manipulative behaviours in the workplace

- ✓ If you have to deal with difficult behaviours, focus on the behaviour, not the person. Saying 'I felt uncomfortable when you criticised my idea' is far less challenging than 'you're being negative'.
- ✓ Cooperate rather than compete, even if the ground rules suggest that competition is the only option. Sometimes workplace values can be shifted by not conforming with the dominant negative feeling.
- ✓ Make sure that you are helpful to all your colleagues, not just the ones who can help you get somewhere.
- ✓ Avoid making critical remarks about colleagues, even if they seem out to get you. You never know how your words will be passed on. Saying nothing is a far easier position to defend.
- ✓ If you have something better to offer than your colleagues, put the focus on your offer rather than on ways of making yourself look better than others.
- ✓ Don't take it personally. You're not the first or the last person to be treated this way.
- ✓ Don't seek revenge. If you do, you've just been manipulated into playing by a whole new set of rules.

How work reputations are built and shaken

'It is better to fail in originality than to succeed in imitation.' **Herman Melville (1850)**

This chapter helps you to:

- Understand how your reputation is shaped and distorted
- Take control of your personal brand as your role develops
- See the difference between conscious and unconscious positioning
- Explore the difference between activity and contribution
- Handle mistakes
- Spot the moment you stop asking and start delivering

Take control of broadcasting house

Inside an organisation, you have a reputation, right from the first day you work there. People are curious about the new kid on the block. They form opinions about whether you're friendly, bright, knowledgeable, confident, perhaps over-confident. They may be pleased to hear your thinking, but will comment to others if you say things were done better in your previous organisation.

To understand how reputations develop, ask yourself a question. When your name comes up in conversation at work, what gets said? Your CV may contain over 200 items of information, but when your name comes up casually, just three or four things are mentioned. In your first few weeks a lot of this is about personality: you're pleasant, energetic, committed; you're curious and ask good questions. Later, other things get tagged on.

Even when we recommend someone, we focus on two or three facts; no one expects a balanced summary. The way we comment on new colleagues is like the way we talk about media personalities – a brief, one-sided perspective. This one-sentence summary can easily be either all positive or all negative. If you're doing OK, you're doing OK – that's often enough as the beginnings of a secure reputation. On the other hand, a throwaway comment that you 'seem out of your depth' is likely to stick.

As a newcomer, you're a puzzle which hasn't yet been cracked. Why have you changed jobs? Are you really the best fit? Any hint that you regret taking the job will quickly become coffee break gossip. Soon people will be saying that you're just marking time until something better comes along.

How do you begin to shape your reputation?

Too many people try to navigate careers without having a grip on how they are seen by others, particularly the people who make decisions about their future. As Chapter 3 outlined, your reputation starts work before you do. Any reputation you acquired in your past will also follow you; people talk to their peers in other organisations. If there are things here you want to adjust, you may need to work even harder at re-crafting your image.

Understanding your internal reputation means you get better traction when you ask for something or propose something new. To understand that reputation, you need an answer to the question: 'How do people see me here?'

How do you find out? If you ask a trusted, friendly colleague, you may hear kindness or flattery. A more objective colleague might give you independent, unbiased feedback – the only kind of feedback you should act on.

A reputation shaped by you

Imagine two senior managers queuing together for coffee. Your name comes up in conversation. The manager who hasn't met you asks what you're like, and how you're getting on – predictable questions.

What do you think comes up next? Answers in this context don't offer all the pros and cons you might see in a detailed performance review. Informally, talking to people we're relaxed with, we answer in simple, binary language: thumbs up or thumbs down.

Let's assume you get a thumbs up. What is said next? When we recommend people, we talk about how they fit in and how they stand out. We don't offer a full overview, but mention things that seem special or different. That's what you hope comes up in this moment – a brief affirmation of why you were hired. Yes, you fit.

However, if the response is a shrug or a wince, something isn't going right. A negative thought has been introduced into the mind of the organisation. If that news reaches you, don't give up hope. Initial responses to new hires are sometimes over-cautious, or based on gut feeling. That can be reshaped.

What gets said in moments like this should not come as a complete surprise. You have a great deal of influence over this conversation. In fact, it's your job to write the script. Nearly every piece of information that pops up when you're not in the room should be generated by you.

Think about the picture you present to others. For example, if in your first weeks of the role you constantly talk about the learning curve being very steep, the mistakes you're making adapting to the new system, or your worry that you're doing everything wrong, those messages become the dominant narrative. On the other hand, if people hear that the learning is exciting, you're relishing new challenges, and getting to grips with new methods, that's what people notice and remember.

Longer-term reputation development

Further down the line you can work at getting more developed messages out there. If your name comes up, what three pieces of information do you really want people to know about? Often these will be very close to the headline information on your CV or LinkedIn page: a few short, positive statements about your skills, expertise, results achieved, projects, organisations, people or systems that you know well. You don't have to sell yourself hard or indulge in an ego trip, just make sure that people know what you've been working on and where you're adding to the agenda.

Personal reputations are built on sound bites like this. Some describe this as *personal branding*. It's an idea that's less popular than it was 20 years ago, largely because it makes people feel they need to sell themselves in an upfront way at every opportunity. It *is* branding in the sense that powerful brands exert power over memory and action – we remember them, choose them again, and recommend them to others. It's great to be recommended – and even better for all the right reasons.

Your reputation is a picture, painted first by you and then recreated daily by other people. Be careful how you shape this picture through your own negativity, verbalising your doubts or running yourself down. Think how easily colleagues start telling each other that you feel swamped by new information and you're finding the job more pressurised than you anticipated.

This book often points to the value of great questions, but they need to be well thought out. If they seem to signal naivety or ignorance, they will sound like floundering rather than intelligent enquiry. Even so, questions which draw out useful information and get to know your colleagues' needs and working styles are infinitely preferable to self-promotion. In general, it's best not to talk too much about yourself in the first few weeks of the role, but to show real curiosity about what people are already doing. Your time will come – when, with careful planning, you bring new ideas to the table, and pitch them well.

As others see you

Being invisible at work (absent, late, not contributing) is a recipe for a negative reputation. A positive reputation can only be built through being visible, and by deciding what features you want to place front and centre in your shop window. We choose what we project.

You may feel relatively content in your role but never say so, meaning that others assume you are unhappy. In contrast, you may feel under-stimulated by work, but your manager thinks you're happy muddling along, and the best strategy is to leave you alone. You may have made some mistakes recently because you no longer find the role demands your full attention. Your manager may read the mistakes as 'underperforming' rather than 'losing interest because the job is over-familiar'. It's important to look at situations from more than one perspective, and be aware how easy it is to lose track of other people's perceptions.

A key step is making your managers feel you are working 'with' them rather than 'against' them. Framing a question in active mode ('how can I help?') sends a very different message to passively expecting instructions ('what do you want me to do now?'). Asking to take something off someone's plate builds alliances much faster than waiting to be allocated work.

Supporting a manager can sometimes mean switching off your idea-filled brain and calmly waiting. Even when you know the answer, it might oil the wheels if you let your manager go through her own thought process, supported by evidence and advice you feed into the discussion. If this sometimes means bosses sound as if your ideas are their own, so be it – making other people look good comes with the territory when you're an effective team member.

Early visibility will often be benchmarked around reliability. Don't arrive late for a meeting – either through complacency or bad planning. If you offer to take something on in your first 100 days, deliver on time (or ahead of time). Bad news travels fast, so failing to deliver even against small promises will be noticed. Another powerful metric is the way you appear to value what other people are doing. In order to be trusted, you need to demonstrate support for others, not just talk about it.

Find out where you can offer quick wins (see Chapter 6) that help others. Make sure the new things you add build on work which has already been undertaken; give credit where it's due (even if it's only half due). Offer fresh opinions and don't feel you have to speak with a corporate voice, but test ideas against organisational reality. Consult, then present. Equally, remain aware of treading on toes. Having a fresh take on things is great, as long as it doesn't sound like a reckless trashing of other people's life work.

It is important to be noticed for the right reasons: positive incidents can create opportunities; negative events can block you for years.

How do you position yourself?

Unconscious positioning	Conscious positioning
Your boss happens to notice you handle a difficult customer well.	You share with your boss what you learned about handling a difficult customer, and ask her advice about doing it even better next time.
You cover someone else's work.	You use the chance of covering for someone else's work to meet new people and ask questions about how another area of work is done.
You learn new skills in your own time.	You aim to apply new skills by seeking opportunities to try out new activities at work which will benefit you employer.
You do something beyond the call of duty.	You record and pass on customer feedback. You also pass on the successful techniques that achieved you the good feedback.
You dislike public praise.	You seek one-to-one feedback on how you can improve, and look for opportunities to share your techniques with others.
You perform tasks to an excellent standard, and you're aware of the short cuts to success.	You share your expertise with others by passing on tips and insights. You are given the chance to train or coach others.

Reframe as you go

Keep helping others to see you more positively, partic-ularly where any part of your reputation is negative.

Since colleagues are wondering why you took the job, particularly if this isn't obvious, you won't help yourself by voicing the same question. Sharing with new team members any concerns you might have about the quality or accuracy of your job description is not to be recommended. Nor is hinting that the job interview oversold the role. If you really believe that you were mis-sold the role, that's not something you should share with an internal audience. Even a wistful 'I really should have been told about. . .' signals a relationship that isn't working. Lacking full information comes with the territory in a new job; you're expected to absorb, adapt, and work things out for yourself.

Focus on the word *respect*. Work cultures intrinsically want to be respected, because they represent an agreed consensus – the tribe's philosophy, if you like, established by habit and resistant to outsider interference. The way things are done may not be the most efficient, but it's a mode of behaviour that has been adopted by a group of people. You gain respect, and permission to contribute, by asking questions which acknowledge this fact.

This is where the art of appreciative enquiry is useful. Appreciative enquiry asks penetrating questions in a positive way. The process begins with a clear single intention: to affirm what's working and build on it in the future. Appreciative enquiry identifies and describes strengths found in existing teams or organisations. Rather than a diagnosis of what is missing or failing, this enquiry considers a future based on what's already working well. So, notice – and praise. Your message needs to be along the lines of 'I can see how this works well, and I look forward to getting involved', rather than 'I've spotted a flaw in the system.' If you discover faults that matter, be careful how you share the news.

The dangers of a solo performance

Workplace image is not achieved in isolation and is strongly connected to the reputation of your team, boss, and organisation. You can shine as an individual, but many people talk about the way that working in a great team was a career boost, or the way that a particular culture and leadership style brought out their talents.

One way of improving your reputation at work is to share information more frequently. Sharing rather than retaining information runs the risk that someone will run off with your ideas, but generally adds to positive team working. Besides, sharing information can often be a subtle way of talking about what you've discovered, learned, and achieved. If you have successes to talk about, focus on how learning from them can help the organisation.

Failures and successes

As you settle into a new role, some things will go right and a few things will go wrong, largely because of your unfamiliarity with new ways of working. Failure may happen because you've set yourself up for a fall, or you've been sabotaged, or you've missed a vital stage in a process. Failure sometimes comes from arrogance – rushing in to a new situation and ignoring advice about the problems you will meet. A classic example is where you are facing an external client or audience and you just don't know enough to be convincing. Do more homework, or shadow someone with the right knowledge.

A second typical situation is where you unwisely accept an opportunity to speak to an audience of fellow workers before you've found your feet (this might of course be an integral part of a leadership role). Take great care – this is like a new kind of selection process, a screen test for the role. In general, what's often appreciated here is honesty about the fact that you're still learning, and plenty of references to the things you've been impressed with. If you tell people how you're going to fix the organisation, you're painting a target on your back. Suspicions that you are an arrogant blow-in are being confirmed.

If you make a big mistake, talk to your manager about it, sooner rather than later. Your reputation has a dent in it. The organisation is now wondering whether hiring you was a major error. Were you faking it at interview? Explore why and how the error happened. Establish the facts carefully, and look hard at the implications of the error: How much damage have you done? How much of it can you fix? Don't rush to blaming others for not providing you with key information or not warning you; it may be your job to judge these situations wisely.

Agree what went wrong, what you learned from the event, and be clear of the steps you will take to avoid repetition. Then get your head down to patch things up – and while you do so, communicate a willingness to take action and work alongside others to solve the problem. Doing so puts the emphasis on your team contribution, rather than the source of the error. You may also discover that some of the high-flyers around you admit to making worse mistakes themselves.

Keep your focus if things go wrong. Avoid allocating blame, either to yourself or someone else. Work out what's gone wrong, find a workable solution, and then review when the pressure is off. Errors are useful; they help you learn a new job more effectively than any handbook or training course. Don't get locked into reflection, and don't keep talking about what went wrong. Mistakes should get as much attention as you need to give them. Be clear about what you learned, and what you would do differently next time. Don't think in circles, reliving moments when you should have said or done something differently.

Review thoroughly, but review once. Set time aside to look at an event, possibly with a coach. Write down *three* things you will do differently next time you face the same problem. If your list has more than three items, it's more about recrimination than action, and you won't put things into effect. Adopt the strategy of 'failing forwards': reflect honestly (but not for too long), learn, then move on. Look for practical changes you can implement quickly. If a meeting didn't go well and you found yourself working with an information blocker (see Chapter 3), think about a different approach, and try that next time.

Monitor apology levels

If you arrive in a large, complicated building in a hurry, you will probably get lost. After a few false turns you start to create an internal map which helps you navigate. In new contexts, we learn – quickly – by making mistakes. As you do so, be careful not to say sorry all the time.

The natural courtesy in a new role is to apologise – for forgetting a procedure, getting a name wrong, not complying with local codes and cultures. You might misread the dress code for a meeting, or not realise that it's your turn to bring lunch or take the minutes. Be careful with how you apologise, and how often. It shows you take responsibility and understand the needs of others, but over-used as a defence strategy it can signal two slightly dangerous things. The first is approval-seeking – asking for forgiveness can easily look like weakness. The second is a kind of insincerity – sometimes people apologise all the time to put other people at ease. Either, in excess, sends out the wrong signals.

Spot when you need to stop consulting and start offering

You will be saying 'I'm here to learn' for a while, but the time when you need to offer answers arrives fairly quickly. You are being judged by two measures simultaneously: whether you fit in, and whether you deliver on promises.

Watch carefully for those moments when someone turns to you and says, 'This is your responsibility now. What do you think?', or 'You've come here with a lot of experience from other organisations. What do you suggest?'

This moment when you really need to offer ideas and answers is a critical moment, one which shapes your reputation. As Chapter 4 suggests, don't sound clueless, or passively ignorant. In week one you might say, 'I haven't got my head round this yet', but you will be expected to have grasped issues within a few weeks. Don't offer glib or unrealistic solutions or suggest that your CV alone makes you a walking solution.

Throw in ideas you'd like people to think about rather than pat answers. Phrases like 'this is something I've tried elsewhere which might be helpful here' land much better than 'my plans are. . .'. Mention conversations that you are looking forward to, an eagerness to test out ideas rather than impose solutions. Project a mix of eagerness, curiosity, and willingness to start things moving, having negotiated cooperation from team members.

All this assumes that you model useful behaviours and demonstrate team fit. Much of this applies even in a junior role: learning fast, asking the right questions but not in excess, and showing quiet competence. On the other hand, if your job is to rattle cages, shake complacency, and weed out under-performers, then say so – don't wrap it up in fake consultation.

Defence strategies to avoid early departure

Anything you can do to improve your profile in a positive way is an action which does something, no matter how small, to keep you off the redundancy list. However, it would be very negative just to stay in survival mode, grimly hanging on to your job, narrowly avoiding career-limiting actions (see Chapter 11). Create a strong impression from your opening moments, then build on it. If you need to do more and reinvent your reputation, Chapter 10 will help.

'Must do' list

- ✓ Work out your starting reputation and how it might need to be adjusted.
- ✓ Monitor what you communicate and the signals it sends.
- ✓ Give more energy to conscious positioning.
- ✓ Plan important conversations carefully, thinking about the perspective of your conversation partner.
- ✓ Think objectively about mistakes and failures, being clear about what you have learned and what you will do differently next time.
- ✓ Observe how often you apologise as a strategy.
- ✓ Watch carefully for the moment when you need to stop asking and start delivering.

Part 2

Beyond the first 100 days

Reinventing yourself

'Anything that takes us out of our comfort zones for a while can act as a reminder that the past we are used to may not be our best future.' **Charles Handy (2015)**

This chapter helps you to:

- Spot times when you might need to reposition yourself
- Rethink when you start working with a new boss
- Refresh your role through 'job sculpting'
- Get an outsider perspective and benchmark your role
- Understand how your future depends on small moments of visibility
- Reinvent yourself to match your ambitions and the organisation's needs

Rebooting

This book looks at your first months in a new role, a vital opportunity to shape how you are seen. There are other times when you might work at adjusting your reputation. For example, it might be that you are transferred or promoted to a new team or division. Or you might stay in the same role and start working for a boss who doesn't know you. Or you might be asked to trial new equipment, software, or procedures. All these situations present opportunities to persuade people to think and talk about you differently – and then recommend you, with evidence, for new reasons. Changing circumstances can offer important opportunities to up your reputation a gear or two.

Is it really possible to 'reinvent' yourself? People do it all the time – when they begin a new role, join a new team, win promotion, or decide to be more visible to attract development opportunities. For example, you might be working in a team and achieve promotion to team leader. You're in a new role, and people need to see you differently.

So, we reinvent. The important thing is to understand who is in charge of this process. By this chapter you will have grasped the idea that your reputation at work is very much shaped by you: you invent, and reinvent, as circumstances demand. Reinventing yourself means consciously repositioning so people start to think about you differently. Turning your back on a moment like this might be a career-limiting action (see Chapter 11).

Strategies for advancement vary widely. The key factors are chemistry and impact – fitting in is important, but so is making the right contribution. Although organisations often talk about skill development, senior managers place high value on attitude and behaviours. Sounding the part is therefore just as important as ticking boxes in appraisals. Key attitudes which help you look like promotable material include a high level of commitment to the organisation, being solutions focused with a 'can-do' attitude, and demonstrating a high degree of flexibility, enthusiasm, and energy. Therefore, to progress in your career you need more than skills and qualities, you need ways of communicating them as behaviours, moments that showcase an attitude to work that mirrors the values of the organisation.

New start with a new boss

Changes of senior staff are frequent. If you get a new manager, see it as the opportunity to reset your reputation. Many people find that having a new boss is a really great opportunity to persuade a whole range of people to see them differently, including their new manager. Helping your manager come on board may give opportunities for you to excel. Be an information broker; offer solutions, not problems, and make an impression fast.

Since a new boss will want an overview of your job, this is your chance to talk about the way you contribute to the big picture. Doing that often means that you can negotiate to do more of the things you do well and enthusiastically, and ask to delegate some tasks you find less interesting.

Sometimes a new boss gives you a chance to rethink your image in a bigger way. Try buying some smart new work outfits, as well as adopting new approaches.

Visible or invisible?

How many times has some recommended that you 'keep your head down and work hard' as an advancement strategy? This is very much a 1960s view of work, when organisations offered long-term job security and well-funded pension schemes.

What's your strategy for moving your career forward? Are you waiting for someone else to move you onto the next rung of the ladder? Hoping your contribution has been noticed? If your strategy is passively hoping and waiting, think again. You can put maximum effort into your job without being noticed, and less effective colleagues may be promoted ahead of you. Working hard is the new norm – people often do this just to hang on to a job. Getting promoted in an age of leaner, flatter organisations needs something else.

Explore role refreshment

Don't complain if your job has become routine and unstimulating. Look at what you can add to it. Investigate learning opportunities, new challenges, or the chance to attach yourself to a new team or project (see Chapter 13 for tips on extending your learning curve). Look for opportunities to refresh not only the work you do but the way you are seen.

Don't expect your manager to do all the running here. No one will magically transform your role, but you can ask to do something different for some of the time. Seek changes to your role which are relatively low risk for the organisation but also make a difference.

If you take on new responsibilities, watch the size of your 'to do' list. Your aim is to ease in interesting tasks, and delegate out unimaginative work. Where an organisation is under-staffed this may seem unrealistic, but it can often be done by increments. It's good to have a road map for the way you'd like your job to develop – one you can come back to in a career conversation (see Chapter 12). If you take on new tasks which prove to be important, your role will probably never revert to what it was. By demonstrating ability and making a distinctive contribution, you may look indispensable and find yourself absorbed into new teams as they develop.

Job sculpting

We often achieve increased job satisfaction when we have some control over the work we do. When tasks become repetitive and you feel you're not learning, you will naturally want to add something new. Broadening your role may be attractive, but of course trying to renegotiate all of your responsibilities can make you seem like a very disgruntled employee.

How do you adapt your role without upsetting your organisation – or risking burn out? One idea that works both for individuals and organisations is the idea of 'job sculpting'. This highly customised form of career management is a tool that can provide an upward trajectory to your learning curve (see Chapter 13), and a useful ingredient in a career conversation.

Essentially, job sculpting is a process where organisations adapt jobs so that they are a better fit for key employees. Sculpting your whole job requires extensive negotiation skills and is hard work, but shaping just parts of it is manageable. Just changing a relatively small part of your role can have significant tangible benefits and can make the experience of work very different.

Every job can be described in terms of three zones (see Figure 10.1). First, the **core zone** – the tasks set out within your job description. If you ignore the basics within the core zone, particularly tasks which matter, you are not only staying in a very low gear but actively undermining yourself. Anyone who simply works to the letter of their job description, adding nothing new to the job, is setting themselves a dangerous career trap.

Next, the **push zone**. This reflects added effort, new ideas, new ways of working and pushing beyond the conventional

Figure 10.1 Job sculpting

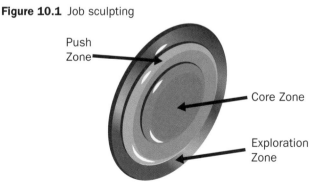

Push Zone

Core Zone

Exploration Zone

boundaries of the role. Reflecting on the push zone is vitally important when it comes to presenting your career evidence. An astute interviewer will have little interest in the basic responsibilities set out in your job description, but will want to know where you brought new ideas to a role or added value.

If you drive a car with the rev counter in the red, you'll damage the engine. The risk of working constantly in the push zone is burn out (see Chapter 12). If you remain in this mode of working, you risk losing focus, and making mistakes, which could be career threatening.

Job sculpting comes into play in the **exploration zone**. This is where you do something different with around 5–10 per cent of your time at work. This might be about learning something new, or being attached to a new project or team. It might involve launching a new idea, writing a white paper, or conducting a feasibility study. The activity might be work which is central to the organisation's main business, or strongly related to organisational values (for example, charity work or a community project).

There are many of ways of sculpting your exploration zone. You might train someone else, or become a mentor. You might add just one new strand to your job description, or make small changes which lead to something bigger, like temporary secondment to another part of the organisation. The reason you focus on 5–10 per cent, a narrow band of change, is because this is small enough to negotiate but big enough to prevent your role becoming stale.

Get a new perspective on your job

Find a way of looking at your job from the perspective of an outsider. Is your contribution to the company clear? Would an outside observer see and value your role, and understand where it fits in? What answer would that same impartial observer have to the question, 'why is this person on the payroll?'

An 'outside-in' perspective can be achieved by bench-marking your role against similar jobs inside the organisation. Is your contribution above or below the norm for others holding an identical job title? Next, benchmark against roles in other organisations. Is your role bigger, more or less complex, than the industry standard? Do roles which have the same job title as yours provide a match in terms of seniority, impact, and status? Don't just look at salary, look at role content.

Talking of job titles, it's important to know if yours holds you back in any way, since this will feature on your CV for some time. Does your job title reflect the complexity and reach of what you do? Are you likely to be pigeon-holed by your current role title? Would your market reputation be improved if you had a different job title? If so, renegotiating what your job is called may be a key step in redesigning your wider reputation. Think also about what you are known for in terms of skills and expertise. If the way you are seen (and recommended) is reducing your market value, this is definitely a time for reinvention.

Look at the cost to your organisation of outside consultants. Are they doing something you can provide? If you can fill the gap, why are you being overlooked? Is there an unchallenged assumption that the best talent lies outside the organisation, or is your 'offer' seen as weak compared with that of outsiders?

How colleagues can help you reinvent

As Chapter 7 outlined, other people can help you get things done. They can also help you get your reputation back in shape.

As we have discussed, personal reputations are built on sound bites just as much as brands. Too many individuals try to navigate their careers without understanding what key decision-makers and influencers think about them. This matters even more if you're trying to build external relationships and hope to be visible in the hidden job market. You have a circle of influence, and within that circle a certain set of messages are passed on in your absence.

Failing to worry about your reputation means you leave it entirely in other people's hands, probably relying on a hackneyed, second-hand, or out-of-date picture of you. Getting inaccurate feedback can send you in the wrong direction. It is also possible to worry too much about your reputation and draw to much attention to it. Investigate, build on your findings, and then leave the issue alone or you will become self-absorbed.

Find insightful support to help you understand what is said about you when your name comes up at senior level. Work hard on reshaping that picture if it fails to point you in the right direction. Take soundings on how you can build on your experience or add to it so that your story fits the one your organisation wants to see.

Try to identify the skills, areas of specialism and knowledge that come up when your name is mentioned in conversation. Here a mentor arguably has greater value than a coach because they are often better at decoding the organisation and providing you with a 'warts and all' picture of how your brand as an employee is seen by others. This helps you understand the things in your reputation you want to adjust or reinforce.

Sometimes you pick this up from passing comments, but it's helpful to receive this as well-structured, positive advice. Trusted colleagues will give you a straight answer to the question: 'What does X think of me?' However, it's often much more useful and appropriate to talk about tasks rather than about you: 'Was there a better way of doing that? How could I have done that differently?'

Who you can consult to get a better picture of how you are seen

- Contacts within the organisation who can tell you the real agenda and the most desired outcomes.
- Trusted colleagues who can provide an unbiased view of the way you are perceived by the organisation.
- A mentor who can provide objective feedback and advice about positioning.
- Honest friends who can tell you about the way you look and sound (don't ignore surface essentials like dressing well, looking smart, sounding alert and sharp, writing and speaking without making major grammatical mistakes).
- People in your organisation who can help your mapping (see Chapter 5) – individuals who know who to talk to and can tell you what's going on.
- Colleagues with particular skills from whom you can learn.
- Colleagues who appear to have strong organisational reputations – what can you learn from their behaviours?
- An independent coach who can help you develop a great communications strategy.
- External contacts who can help you learn from other organisations in the same sector.

Micro-visibility – how decisions are made about your future

As we noted at the start of this chapter, some workers believe they will be offered a promotion if they put in a strong, year-round work performance. If they work effectively and consistently for 12 months of the year, they expect this to be considered when advancement opportunities are made available. They believe this contribution is on record, and that positive appraisals will naturally lead to positive change.

It is, of course, perfectly possible to work very hard and to be ignored when it comes to promotions. When this happens you might be baffled – what else could you possibly do to get noticed? What is the intangible, unreachable 'something extra' that gets other people noticed? Yes, it is true that some people achieve advancement because they are noticed – but these moments of visibility may be much briefer than you think.

When you talk to people who have achieved interesting promotions and found themselves in exciting roles, you will discover that reputations are shaped and built by micro-visibility. Your name comes up not as a result of year-round performance, but because of flash moments where key individuals saw you do something significant. Because you shone for a few minutes, important people saw you in a suddenly different and positive light. Micro-visibility is therefore about tiny moments where your contribution is noticed by people who matter.

Look back at the last 12 months and think about moments where you were observed by senior staff, or your work was presented to them in some way. If you made a strong impression, your currency rises. You're remembered for a succinct verbal report you delivered to a board meeting. You worked on a highly visible project. You shone on a secondment or when covering for a manager. Your name comes up regularly and your attitude is seen to be positive. Working hard provides impact, but it's far less powerful than controlled visibility.

You won't always be able to engineer these peak moments of visibility, but you should be prepared to cash in on them. You may find that by chance the CEO happens to be in the room when you're presenting an exciting idea or reporting on a successful project. Get the best out of these moments by always having some good sound bites and clear positive summaries in your toolkit.

Naturally, you shouldn't passively rely on chance, waiting for these moments to arise. Make conscious decisions to create and manage opportunities that enhance visibility. This might be about writing a key document, making an important presentation to colleagues, taking an idea to senior management, or being seen to be highly focused on the agenda central to the organisation. If you're in any way uncertain what that agenda is, go back to Chapter 4.

Decisions about your future therefore happen through micro-visibility – small moments with big consequences. What these moments have in common is that they are noticed, and have the right audience. Think about doing things that are pretty much guaranteed to get you noticed. Volunteer for pilot schemes, multi-disciplinary projects, and new teams. Track the issues and ideas that appear to matter most to your present employer, and find opportunities to get involved.

Learn the difference between activity and contribution: don't just work hard, *work hard on the things that matter*. Put your best energy into projects and issues that are being discussed at the highest level in your organisation. Don't just gather information, understand what weighting to give it. Find a mentor who is senior and wise enough to decode the business for you.

Meetings with senior managers

It's hardly worth pointing out that you need to think and plan before a meeting with a senior decision-maker, particularly if this opportunity arises within the first few months of starting. Use this contact time carefully and imaginatively. Remember that this may be the first time that this senior manager has heard your voice or seen what you can do. Up to now you may have just been a face or a name. The first impression you make here will be as important as the initial impact you might make in a job interview, except here the stakes could be even higher.

Think carefully about why you are there. Is it simply to say hello and introduce yourself? If so, put all your effort into building a warm relationship. Otherwise, be clear of your agenda. Are you in the room to ask a question, convey information, or put forward an idea? Are you looking for a viewpoint, a steer, or a decision?

If your role here is to provide input, plan your message carefully and deliver it concisely. Know where you can put your hands on back-up information in case you need it. If this is the first time this manager has met you, clarity along with calm professionalism will make a powerful starting impression. Briefly summarise what you've already discovered through research or enquiry – show you don't need spoon-feeding. Make it very clear from the outset what outcome you are looking for: 'I'd like your view about . . .' or 'I wonder if you can give me a decision on . . .?'

If the meeting happens close to your start date, avoid asking questions which sound basic. Don't ask for information that you could have obtained from this manager's subordinate, or worse still from a document that is sitting in your inbox. Don't apologise or say you're not fully up to speed yet. You won't be expected to know everything, but you will be expected to have a focus on critical tasks. Confirm details in writing, if appropriate in a follow-up email. In general, it pays to over-deliver against anything you have committed to during this initial meeting. Failure to deliver on these first set tasks will almost certainly put you on the wrong side of a 'set-up-to-fail' decision (see Chapter 11).

Communicating your reinvented self

This book has argued that your career really gets on track when you find a genuine trade-off between your goals and the current anxieties and vision of your employer. But you also need to know how to communicate the key ingredients in your deal – what you do well, how you'd like to be remembered, and how you see your future.

Communicating these points to an organisation is essentially a strong piece of marketing. You have a clear sense of your offer, and a clear sense of your audience. You understand your present impact on that audience because you have a strong grasp of how you are already seen. You have ideas about how you want to change that perception. If you want to reinvent yourself, start putting those ideas into action.

'Must do' list

- ✓ Talk to others in your organisation who have achieved promotion or career enhancement, and learn from their strategies.
- ✓ If you get a new boss, review your working style, image, and impact.
- ✓ Work with a mentor or trusted colleague to get an outsider perspective on your role and your reputation.
- ✓ Seek out, or take advantage of, moments where you will achieve micro-visibility.
- ✓ If your role has gone stale or doesn't match your main drivers and motivators, negotiate positive changes.
- ✓ When negotiating role adjustments, be clear how the organisation benefits.
- ✓ When you've decided on your reinvented self, work out the best ways to communicate your offer.

11

Career traps

'Management is efficiency in climbing the ladder of success; leadership determines whether the ladder is leaning against the right wall.' **Stephen R. Covey (1989)**

This chapter helps you to:

- Understand how career traps operate, and how to avoid them
- Look at the emotional impact of your role
- Monitor whether you're being set up to fail
- Dodge the poisoned chalice
- Identify career-limiting actions
- Ensure the organisation sees you as a vital asset

Watching for traps

Your career trajectory will be shaped by the new role you've just taken on, and it may rise or fall more quickly than you imagine. Decisions might be made about your future before you've even finished reading your induction material. As we have learned, the first 100 days in your new role are critical in setting your career along the right path.

Down the line, you might encounter other blocks to career progress. These can take the form of career 'traps' – events or situations which hold you back, reduce job satisfaction, and sometimes push you closer to the exit.

Career traps can arise from external circumstances, difficult colleagues, or confused goals, but we're also capable of sabotaging our own careers without much help. Traps are sometimes obvious, and these include inappropriate behaviours. Avoid language or attachments in office email that you wouldn't be comfortable sharing with your grandparents. For sheer self-protection, think twice before pressing 'send' on any email that says something difficult or forceful.

Other career traps are rather more subtle – the booby traps we lay for ourselves when we are actively trying to do the right things. Traps might be about knowledge: failing to keep your knowledge relevant and up to date, aligning yourself with out-of-date systems, or making casual comments about how things used to be done. Traps are set when you demonstrate attitudes considered unhelpful to the organisation.

Sticking rigidly to your job description is perhaps the biggest career trap of all, marking you as inflexible and lacking interest in role development. Career traps are usually avoided by working smarter, not harder – placing energy where it's most effective. Keep the changing needs of your organisation in mind. Monitor your company's biggest issues and initiatives, as if your life savings were invested in it.

Other traps are avoided by anticipating the emotional impact of your work. Whose toes are you treading on when you suggest new working methods? Who will be irritated by innovation? Whose pet project are you trashing by proposing change? Learn how to spot the minefields, and you might just have a chance to navigate a way through them.

Any remaining career traps are usually about your boss. Take solutions to your manager more often than you take problems. Don't always double-check every instruction or hope to be 100 per cent fireproof – learn when to take risks. If you do something that irritates your boss on a daily basis (perhaps you believe that a tidy desk is a sign of a sick mind), get over yourself and do things differently.

Being set up to fail

A classic career trap opens when you take on a role that has demanding targets but inadequate resources to enable success. Worse still, you may have a manager who is not only convinced you will fail, but is unconsciously making sure that you do.

Senior managers seem to make early, half-conscious decisions about new hires. This is described by Manzoni and Barsoux in *The Set-Up-To-Fail Syndrome* (2002). The book has the revealing subtitle, 'How good managers cause great people to fail'. The authors claim that managers decide early whether new appointees will succeed or fail. There is little middle ground: you're either seen as a probable 'star', or someone unlikely to have a long-term future and not worth investing in. This decision about potential winners and losers is instinctive and often made after minimal contact.

Then the problem deepens. Managers act on their first hunch by allocating plum tasks to those who look like future stars, and by giving less exciting projects to others. Additionally, they are more likely to give positive feedback to favoured staff, allocating others tasks where it is much harder to shine. The theory also suggests that managers unconsciously undermine the performance of non-stars through ineffective feedback and weak interventions, or by putting them in situations where failure is inevitable. This results in a downward spiral of negative feedback and perception. Manzoni and Barsoux write: 'The subordinate sees the boss as intransigent, interfering, and hypercritical; the boss sees the subordinate as inept, uncooperative, and indecisive. They are well and truly caught up in the set-up-to-fail syndrome' (p. 7).

A textbook example is where a manager always delegates to your weaknesses rather than to your strengths, or allocates tasks where in the past others have struggled. You may find yourself in a cycle which ends up with a negative appraisal and a reputation for incompetence.

Creating the right initial impression with a manager is therefore vital. Judgements are made on the first few occasions you are noticed. A set-up-to-fail decision may be happening in those first few weeks when everyone smiles benevolently as you struggle to learn new systems. You think your progress is acceptable and largely unseen, unaware that you're in an audition for a part on the main stage.

When beginning a role (or working with a new boss), signal focus, competence, and enthusiasm. Be clear as you take on a job what problems need to be solved quickly, and the skills which demonstrate above-average competence. Try to get a picture of what your line manager sees as the most important reason you were offered the job.

Ten classic career traps

Trap 1: Being flattered into accepting a promotion

You may feel pressurised to apply for an internal position, since someone suggests you would be 'perfect for the job'. You don't want to let down the person making the recommendation, particularly if it's somebody you respect. The difficulty with an internal position is that taking it without reflection is dangerous, but turning down a promotion or transfer can also damage your reputation.

Check out any new opportunity carefully, without sounding negative. Make sure it is a good match, and a good stepping stone. If it's not, don't sound ungrateful. Offer a positive reason for deciding to stay where you are for the moment, or talk about alternative ideas for career development.

Trap 2: Hitting the ceiling

The term 'glass ceiling' is probably familiar. It's an invisible barrier preventing some people from progressing upwards. Women often feel that they hit a glass ceiling in terms of pay and promotion. Others may hit a glass ceiling, too – non-graduates, for example. To break through this kind of barrier, mine the experience of others who have done it before you. Look for strategies you can adapt to work for you.

Where the glass ceiling is set around certain kinds of qualifications or experience, you face the same problem as a job applicant. Seek out and encourage exceptions to the rule book; find examples of people who have navigated round obstacles. If your employer sets a requirement you cannot meet, ask why the restriction exists, and show how you are a good match in other ways. For example, if you're told that only graduates get to a certain pay grade, explain how your training and experience are more valuable than a paper qualification. Glass ceilings have no rational basis; if they did, they would be stated policy rather than unstated reality.

Trap 3: Becoming over-specialised

Specialist expertise is valued by organisations, but not necessarily in senior staff. It's a difficult balancing act. Being seen as a specialist has its upside – being the 'go to' person on a particular issue or software package can flag you as an indispensable asset. On the other hand, having a narrow focus to your work can be a plus for a while but in the longer term can close down your options (also see Chapter 6).

The job may require specialised know-how and skills, but it's often best to adopt these on a project-by-project basis and move on each time to new challenges. Specialist knowledge may be vital if you intend to develop a portfolio or consultancy career, or in order to progress in technical roles in certain industries. In a general management role, it's often unwise to over-specialise because it can limit you to one area of the business.

Those with highly specialised profiles sometimes find it hard to step into the very top jobs. Often, those rising to very senior positions are knowledgeable generalists, but this is not always the case.

The key issue is not what's on your CV, but how you are seen. If your specialism isn't central to the business, you will be seen as an eccentric, working hard on projects that don't really matter. It can also lock your career in a particular gear; if you're known for one thing only, it's easy for others to assume that's all you want to do, and all you will do in the future.

Trap 4: Being stuffed into the wrong pigeon-hole

Being seen as a one-trick performer is a form of 'pigeon-holing', a term that describes how people are labelled at work. Sometimes this is stereotyping ('bureaucrat') or insulting ('geek'). This picture of you could be out of date, based on a role you held some time back. If the label you're known by is a poor fit, this can block your career. The best way forward is to challenge assumptions: 'I expect you think I'm mainly interested in research. Actually, I've really enjoyed some of the training I've been doing recently . . .'.

There is a positive version of pigeon-holing – where the label is accurate. Your career starts to take off when your reputation is accurate as well as positive. The things you're know for are the things you want people to remember. If people recommend you for the right reasons, the hidden job market begins to open up for you.

Trap 5: Accepting the poisoned chalice

Sometimes you are flattered into taking a role that turns out to be full of problems. If you're offered a new role, spot the warning signs itemised below.

Signs that the job is a poisoned chalice

- Change is necessary, but the person who institutes it is unlikely to survive in the job. Check this one out by finding out why change is necessary and who has a vested interest in opposing it.
- The job is unwinnable – objectives are confused or conflicting.
- The job is seriously under-resourced in terms of staff, budgets, or both.
- The role reports to two managers or more with conflicting styles or objectives.
- No one has lasted in the job for more than 12 months.
- Your role is so ringed around by rules, restrictions, or bureaucracy that you'll be swamped with paperwork from day one.
- People affected by the job have vested interests and want to preserve the status quo.
- Your new boss hates people who seem more talented or success-ful than him.
- The job can't be done by someone who also needs to sleep and have any kind of relationships outside work.

Trap 6: Taking on a challenge without the resources to succeed

A similar career trap opens up when you take on a role that has demanding targets but does not have the matching level of resources to allow you to succeed. Explore the resources available to you, and find out how these problems are nor-mally solved. If you didn't negotiate this before you took the role, this would be a good time to check in with your line manager. Rather than asking 'How do I do this?', ask 'How would you like this done?'

Trap 7: Failing to manage change

Almost every job you can imagine in today's economy is about change. Technology doubles in power every 12 months or so. Organisations grow, shrink, and reinvent themselves. Managing change is part of every job, but expressly so for anyone who manages staff or resources.

'Managing change' is a buzz phrase you will see in both CVs and job descriptions. The reality is that if you do manage change, you may be just 24 hours away from the next crisis. And that's the point – managing change is a process, not an event. You can sometimes pat yourself on the shoulder for making change happen, but the satisfaction will be short-lived.

The key characteristics of people who move from one change process to the next are widely recognised: resilience, flexibility, and a generally positive mindset that believes there is a way forward, a work-around, and the next crisis will be no worse than the last. Sounding as if you're enjoying the ride, just a little at least, is a key attitude. Looking as if each round of change is hammering you deeper and deeper into a hole is an unguarded request for your organisation to replace you.

Trap 8: Failing to manage others

If you are working in a line management capacity, be wary of falling into the career trap of being seen as a poor manager. This, again, is a matter of perception rather than reality. Your superiors probably won't have first-hand experience of your style as a manager or supervisor, but they will judge you by the results of your team, and by the number of problems that are generated along the way. Be aware that the performance of your subordinates reflects on you, and also that a good, productive relationship with your team may be taken as a benchmark for progress. Or, in other terms: be careful how you treat people on your way up! A fairly clear sign of difficulties is where you cause above-average staff retention problems, or staff regularly complain about you to other managers. You will also be judged by the quality of the staff you recruit and appoint.

What management style works best? There are endless books written on this topic, but one big idea stands out: whatever your management style, whether tyrant, coach, or guru, *be consistent.* Nothing disturbs staff like having to second guess which way up you're going to be in the morning.

Trap 9: Getting into a rut

A career rut is a state of inertia. You recognise the symptoms when you are in one: you have probably stopped learning, your job offers few challenges, and your motivation to undertake tasks you have done before decreases every month. Why don't you get out of the rut? Because it's a *velvet rut* – a rut that is just a little too comfortable to get out of. The money's good, you have an easy journey to work, and a new role may not be as exciting as it seems . . .

Being in a rut can be a career trap because we start to lose awareness of our lack of energy and contribution. In a way, we become a little too relaxed about our performance. We start to take pride in the fact that we don't need to learn new-fangled ideas or techniques. We begin to lose touch with what's going on in our company and outside it in our industry.

The beginnings of an escape from this trap are found in two questions: What happens if nothing changes? And what can I adjust right away?

Trap 10: Fear of getting things wrong

Trying to do everything perfectly is a flawed strategy. The pace of work means that you need to learn to deliver 'good enough' most of the time rather than lingering over the details and always producing perfection. The exception is when it really matters – when you (or your boss) need to look good.

As Chapter 9 outlines, mistakes require and enable us to learn. Gardeners learn from the plants they kill. Avoiding all mistakes means avoiding risk, and most jobs involve controlled risk of some kind. Work out the difference between times where a mistake means failure (failing to book an air ticket, or missing a despatch deadline) and times when a mistake means that you learn to think and act differently. Being seen as a 'safe pair of hands' is often about responding under pressure flexibly, knowing when to check details, and knowing when to play the odds.

Getting bogged down in the small stuff often means that you miss the big picture – the stuff that really matters. This is why perfectionists can get passed over for promotion – they are busy checking the fine print on projects that don't really matter. Many businesses run on the principle of deciding on the thing that looks approximately right, and committing to it – trying to be 100 per cent right, 100 per cent of the time, simply locks you into indecision.

Remember that hanging your reputation on perfection is a tough call – one slip, which may be out of your control, and your record's smashed. It's easy to spend too much time focusing on things that have gone wrong. As Chapter 9 outlines, reviewing where you made an error is useful, and accepting blame where it falls on your shoulders is a sign of an adaptive mindset, but don't get locked into one event, turning a road bump into a tank trap.

Think of other qualities that will get you promoted even if you do make small mistakes: being adaptable to circumstances, coming up with creative solutions, focusing on the projects that are closest to the hearts of decision-makers.

Career-limiting actions

As you become more attuned to your organisation and ways of steering a successful path through it, avoiding classic career traps, you will become more aware of the factors that make you successful. You'll also see that some activities and behaviours have exactly the opposite effect. Some of these can be described as career-limiting actions. Review how many of these have got in the way for you in the past.

Career-Limiting Actions

A. Tasks and people

DON'T limit yourself to your job description and refuse to go beyond it.

DON'T be over-competitive. Being competitive is fine, but climbing over the backs of others to reach your personal goals will be widely resented (see Chapter 8).

DON'T gossip and criticise. It may make you entertaining in coffee breaks, but doesn't position you as someone who can be trusted to bring out the best in others.

DON'T hog the credit. Share it. Make sure your boss know who else is working well. If your boss wants the credit, live with that sometimes.

DON'T fail to delegate – ideally, you should be training up your successor.

B. Your boss

DON'T fail to observe your boss's style. Don't just do what your boss wants, but do it in the way he or she wants it done.

DON'T feed your boss's pet hates. Work out the behaviours which irritate your boss, and stop them. It's worth the personal struggle, and allows you to negotiate over things that really matter.

DON'T forget the stuff your boss values – whether it's telephone numbers or the names of her children!

C. Processes

DON'T put too much or too little in writing. Each organisation has its own internal rules on the use of email to confirm decisions. Learn what is acceptable and necessary, and always do it with a light touch rather than sounding bossy.

DON'T fight the bureaucrats. Upsetting those people who want you to fill in Form H76T by Wednesday only adds to negative messages about you. Bite the bullet; fill the form in, and move on.

DON'T hold long and unnecessary meetings. People love short, focused meetings – and rarely get them.

D. Attitudes and behaviours

DON'T dress like you've lost interest. Dress like someone the next grade up, not like someone two weeks from retirement.

DON'T say NO to everything. Learn to say no, but as positively as you can (see Chapter 8). Don't say no just out of habit or survival instinct.

DON'T say YES to everything either. Over-committing leads to under-performance, and gives you the reputation of someone who doesn't deliver.

DON'T take your moods to work. Try to maintain a reasonably consistent, friendly style. Smile. It helps.

DON'T get out of touch with your industry. Happily admitting you are no longer up to date and using phrases like 'in my time . . .' clearly marks you as disposable goods.

DON'T take criticism or rejection personally. New ideas get shot down all the time. Learn to bounce back.

DON'T communicate badly, especially in writing. Take care to check documents and emails for glaring errors and ambiguity.

How disposable an asset are you?

Think of yourself as a corporate asset: a building, a piece of equipment, a vehicle. Disturbing isn't it? Suddenly you feel much more disposable. Companies boast that their people are their greatest asset, but often it seems like people are their greatest *disposable* asset. We dispose of things (gadgets, equipment, vehicles, buildings, information) when:

1. We haven't used them for a while.
2. They don't contribute directly to success.
3. They're a headache.
4. We can't remember why we got them in the first place.

Organisations make staff redundant for many reasons – restructuring, mergers, or changing market fortunes. Sometimes organisations use these circumstances as an excuse to get rid of people who don't fit – those who fit one or more of the categories above.

What can you do to keep yourself out of this career trap? Realise that the need to communicate your strengths within an organisation isn't just about achieving advancement. Sometimes it's about keeping your job. And it's always about being seen as an asset making a direct and visible contribution.

'Must do' list

- ✓ Identify career traps you and others have experienced. What traps are you most likely to fall into in the next two years?
- ✓ If you feel you're being set up to fail, what steps can you take to adjust the way key decision-makers view your future?
- ✓ Review the ten Classic Career Traps described above. Which ones are most likely to affect you? What can you do to avoid them?
- ✓ Review career-limiting actions that have affected your past. What steps can you take to avoid making similar mistakes?
- ✓ Work with a coach or mentor to find better ways of signalling that you're a useful asset.

12

Surviving, thriving, and negotiating change

'My mission in life is not merely to survive, but to thrive; and to do so with some passion, some compassion, some humour, and some style.' **Maya Angelou (2011)**

This chapter helps you to:

- Review the way you accept challenges and what gets in the way of success
- Gain focus to see where your contribution has most traction
- Get the most out of working with a mentor
- Avoid the risks of rust out and burn out
- Plan for a structured career conversation
- Develop negotiating strategies for changing your role

As you become established in a role, you will want to build on your first 100 days. This chapter looks at strategies and behaviours which move you from simply keeping your head above water, to a position where you make an impact. From that point you may move into a phase where you start to add weighty new evidence to your CV. First, you survive and, eventually, you thrive.

Accept challenges, but thoughtfully

Moving on from survival mode is often about responding to critical incidents. Be careful the first time you're given a difficult challenge. Find time to talk about what you need to get from A to B. This isn't about being unrealistic about resources – most people would like more help and more time – or appearing needy. Failing to consider the tools you need to complete the job is about setting yourself up for a fall.

If it's complicated and will take you more than a few hours to achieve, it's reasonable to scope the task out properly. It's often useful to summarise the key outcomes back to the person delegating the work to you. You may also need to negotiate the time you need, and agree what other work can be dropped for the moment.

Look at what you need to get the job done. This could be about direct resources such as equipment and people, but often the support you will need will be in terms of learning (how you acquire or develop relevant skills and knowledge). You may also need support in terms of supervision. Learn to do this with a light touch: 'I hope it's all right for me to check in with a progress report early next month?' With people you know and trust you can be even more explicit about your need for encouragement ('do tell me if I'm doing OK or making a mess of things . . .').

Communicating what you do best

Working hard, even if it's on key objectives, may not be sufficient. Doing a good job, in a pressurised environment, is rarely enough. You need to show how you have added value, solved a problem, or rescued a project. You need to be spotted by at least one person in an influential position. Your contribution needs to be focused, visible, and noticed (see Chapter 10 on micro-visibility).

This sounds like a recipe for boasting, but in fact the technique to use is information sharing. Rather than listing your achievements as outcomes, share the route you took so others can adopt the same approach. Put more emphasis on the *how* than the *what* – tell people about the strategy you adopted.

Sometimes the most effective strategy is to identify what your organisation needs, move into that area, and focus your attention only on the points where visible impact can be achieved. This often means building relationships with those who can help you do what you do best, and finding opportunities for exposure in your areas of competence.

Work with a mentor

Mentors do important things in today's workplace. Sometimes an organisation has a formal mentoring programme. More frequently, however, staff find their own mentors, either inside or outside the organisation.

Having a mentor inside the organisation has powerful benefits. The ideal internal mentor is someone more senior than you who can (a) decode the organisation better than you, and (b) provide an objective picture of how well you fit. A mentor is someone who can tell you whether people wince or smile when your name comes up. They help you understand promotion criteria (both the official process and the unwritten rules).

An internal mentor can reveal how others – especially decision-makers – see your contribution. Discover what gets said about you when your name comes up at senior level. Work hard on reshaping that picture if it fails to point you in the right direction. A mentor helps you see yourself from the perspective of a neutral observer, judging how well you perform and what else you need to do to make an impact.

The disadvantage of a mentor inside the organisation is that, unless there are very clear boundaries set from the outset, objectives may become blurred. If your mentor is involved in decisions about your future development or promotion, for example, or asked for an internal reference, then role conflict arises.

An external mentor can sometimes give even more impartial advice about progression, renegotiating your role, and will usually provide valuable help when you're considering moving on (see Chapter 13) and wondering how marketable you are. Where your mentor has in-depth industry knowledge, this helps enormously when you're benchmarking yourself against others in your sector.

The disadvantage of working with a mentor outside your organisation, unless they were recently employed within it, is a lack of familiarity with people and systems.

What gets in the way of success for you?

This important coaching question can flag up many simple factors which make the difference between surviving and thriving in a new role. When you look at the road blocks to getting things done and building a reputation, they might include external constraints, budget, organisational culture, and a range of other things outside your control. If you ask the question 'what ensures success, and what gets in the way?', there is usually a one-word answer: *people*.

Typical things getting in the way of success in the workplace include functional matters such as poor communication or planning, or tasks that are not matched to appropriate resources. However, people factors are more common, including management style (being micro-managed, or left to flounder, plus managers who do not set clear goals or manage using a consistent style). People issues often relate to relationships within and between teams, such as unhealthy competition, information blocking, and silo behaviours.

In other words, thriving in a role often involves understanding how relationships assist or block progress. Look back at Chapter 7 at the way relationships impact on your work performance and image, and review Chapter 8 for a closer look at toxic work cultures.

Rust out and burn out

This chapter has looked at times when you are put under pressure. As you become more comfortable and the job becomes more routine, the pressures may decrease. However, developments may increase stress and lengthen your working hours. Operating with your rev counter in the red zone, like driving with the pedal on the floor, may be acceptable in an emergency or for very short periods of time, but can easily become 'business as usual'. When one crisis overlaps another, burn out is a likely outcome. The symptoms may be more apparent to your family than to you – exhaustion, being distracted, staying locked into work mode during weekends and holidays.

We're all familiar with the psychological effects of burn out, but don't always recognise the career impact. The problem about working in a fast gear continually is that fatigue reduces the quality of decision-making and diminishes your effectiveness. You're more likely to make mistakes, or to expend vital energy on irrelevant issues.

If you think you're at risk of burn out, look for a positive intervention. This might be a session with a mentor, a programme of coaching, or an honest conversation with your manager. The key question to ask yourself is: 'What happens if nothing changes?' – what happens to your health, wellbeing, and relationships at home?

The other risk is *rust out* – where you're performing the same tasks repeatedly, lacking variety in your work, and you've stopped learning. Workers experiencing rust out often say that their role no longer stretches them. As you will learn in Chapter 13, when you hit the top of your learning curve, a period of stasis can follow. This can prompt relief in the short term, but in the long term lack of stimulation in a job can easily make people cynical under-performers. Getting stuck in a role which adds nothing to your learning, providing no variety or new challenges, is a fairly effective career trap, especially if your lack of engagement becomes obvious to others. If your career is at risk of rust out, it's probably time for a conversation.

Moving towards your first appraisal

Conversations about roles can be informal, but are sometimes structured and scheduled. The best known variant is the appraisal.

Appraisals have their limitations. Some workers find them stressful and unproductive (interestingly, many managers feel the same way). If the discussion focuses entirely on past results, little may be said about your future. They may be weak tools for improving performance or dispensing praise, especially if there's a long gap between meetings. Sometimes the feedback given feels both negative and vague (being told you can do better but without concrete examples); for others, it's simply an exercise in form filling.

In skilled hands, an appraisal can be objective and constructive. It can tell you if your idea of impact and success matches that of the organisation, and can help you identify areas for personal development. Sometimes these conversations can be good ways of thinking about your career.

Plan carefully for your first appraisal. The process needs decoding with care. Enquire informally: find out how appraisals are performed, and how much weight is attached to them. Ask for information about the way the meeting will be structured, and what you need to prepare in advance. Find hard evidence to show how you have met any objectives set for you, and come up with suggestions for future activity.

Remember the advice in Chapter 6 about objectives and outcomes. It's easy to assume that an appraisal simply ticks boxes about objectives achieved. There's a lot more going on. Think about the human impact of what you're presenting. Does your contribution to the meeting sound like a complaint? Are you presenting solutions alongside problems?

People remember feelings longer than facts. For example, making your boss look good, snatching victory from the jaws of defeat, winning back an unhappy client – these become core narratives that can shape your future.

Plan in advance for the way you will deal with any negative feedback. Don't let your personality get in the way, and don't blame others or 'the system' for your mistakes. Remember the advice in Chapter 9 about apologising. If you begin by listing results you haven't delivered, the meeting will go downhill from the start.

Building on appraisals

The main reason for looking at appraisals is to explore the opportunities they offer for talking about your career. Some organisations value appraisals very highly and use them as a finely tuned tool for nurturing talent. In these circumstances, appraisals will naturally look at any gap that exists between someone's career expectations and the role they presently occupy.

All work is a deal, and every deal needs a regular review of terms. A *career conversation* has a range of special characteristics. It looks at what you expected when you joined the organisation, and how far those expectations have been met. It looks at the ways you have grown and changed. It formulates a personal development plan. It looks at strategies for protecting and improving your future within the organisation. You're looking for a two-way exchange of feedback and ideas. Therefore, at least half of the responsibility for outcomes lies with you.

At the end of your first 100 days your organisation may instigate a review, particularly if you need to achieve a formal sign-off at the end of a three-month probation period. This may be a perfunctory 'box-ticking exercise' or a more considered and thoughtful review, depending on the culture and practice of your organisation. In a role new to you, it may still be wise to ask for a brief review after six months – just checking in, making sure you're on track. After 12 months you're probably ready for a career conversation. If this doesn't happen routinely in your organisation, ask for one anyway. You won't be alone. Many organisations now regularly survey employee engagement levels, and in the process often learn that employees would value career conversations (especially where organisations have become flatter, with less obvious opportunities for promotion).

Without career development, people can begin in roles which seem interesting, but eventually feel under-challenged. This can easily lead to an unhelpful mix of boredom and guilt because motivation levels are dropping. The danger of course is that you move on to a new role for the wrong reasons. Or you become unproductive and cynical – and thus high up the next list of redundancies.

Planning for a career conversation

Set the meeting up carefully. If your boss hates surprises, pitch your case in writing before you meet. Do your homework: discover where other people have negotiated changes to their jobs, been offered learning opportunities or secondments.

Be clear: you're looking for a *conversation*, not a moaning session. Managers find it deeply unsatisfying when workers talk vaguely about decreased job satisfaction – this is something they generally find difficult to fix. If you say you're bored, you may be given more work, not more interesting tasks. Don't ask for impossible outcomes, expecting your manager to wave a magic wand and solve all your problems.

Don't go anywhere near this kind of discussion without clear evidence of what you've added to your role in the last 12 months, and where you have made a distinctive contribution. Use the **15-Minute Career Audit** in Chapter 13 to identify highlights. Talk about problems, how you approached them, and outcomes.

Planning for a career conversation

Here are some questions to ask yourself:

- What did I expect from my role? How have these expectations been met in reality?
- What skills have I been using most? How can I develop them?
- What skills and know-how do I want to acquire in the future?
- What kind of challenges would I enjoy?
- What experiences do I want to add to my CV?
- Which teams or individuals or projects would I like to work with?
- How might I be able to reduce or delegate tasks I find demotivating?
- What quick wins can I offer?
- What project ideas, initiatives, or pilot studies can I suggest?
- How can I communicate the benefits of these ideas to my employer?
- Who do I need to convince?
- What's the best way of making my case to my employer?

Career conversations don't work if you expect to be given all the answers. Make positive suggestions about how your job might grow or change. Investigate opportunities, and offer matching solutions. Make your ideas concrete, realistic, and – if necessary – budgeted, always showing how the organisation benefits. You will find this win/win flavour in the RESET career conversation model below.

The RESET career conversation

RECAP

As the discussion begins, recap your reasons for asking for it. Explain why this conversation matters to you, and how you think it might be useful.

'The reason I asked for this conversation is . . .'

EXPECTATIONS

Outline your personal expectations when you started the role, and how things have worked out in practice. Keep things positive.

'When I started the job I thought I would be mainly focused on legacy projects, and it's been a pleasant surprise to be asked to kick-start some new work . . .'

Say a little about what the organisation has expected from you to date:

'I've been asked to rethink our customer service programme, and as you know I've just gained approval for the new package.'

SKILLS AND THEIR IMPACT

Do your homework in advance. Make a record of your top skills and where you have used them. Think about the tasks and contexts which motivate you and your preferred working style. Think about what you'd like to learn in the short-term future.

You might want to set these out in writing in advance. Summarise them in the discussion.

'These are the main skills I've been using, and where I've applied them.'
'I really enjoy . . .'
'I get a buzz out of . . .'
'I'd like the chance to do more . . .'

In terms of impact, outline how you've made a contribution to your organisation in the last 6–12 months. What has your main contribution been? How have you made a difference or added value?

List ways you've gone beyond your job description, made a difference, and added value. Discuss tasks you were allocated, and areas where you've taken the initiative.

EXPLORATION

Suggest exploratory ideas for change – new tasks and responsibilities you might take on, new learning, new opportunities.

Present one or two really good ideas for adapting your role that (a) make your job more interesting and (b) make a strong and measurable contribution to the organisation. Make sure you explain how your ideas work for you and for the organisation – in WIN/WIN terms.

'If you'd like to get the best value out of me, I'd love the chance to . . .'
'This is what I'd like to learn . . .'
'This is what I'd like to take on . . .'
'Here's something I've identified that draws on my primary skills . . .'
'This is how the organisation will benefit . . .'

TRACKED RESULTS

Agree what happens next and who takes responsibility. Look at actions that need to be taken, areas for investigation, and the need for conversations with other people. Try to ensure that both parties in the conversation agree to action. If you agree changes, be clear what they are and how they are initiated.

Track the results of this conversation: be clear about next steps and who is accountable for them. Agree a review date.

'OK, so this is what I think I need to do next . . .'
'It would be great if you could help me by . . .'
'Can we put a meeting in the diary to review progress on this?'

Know what you're asking for

Think about what you want to happen as a result of this conversation. Do you want to change the focus of your role? Learn something new? Work with a different project or team? Achievable outcomes might include role development, learning opportunities, the chance to work with another team or to be seconded to another part of the organisation, or in fact any step which helps you the experience and responsibility you need to move up the career ladder.

If you're looking for a promotion, say so – don't assume it's obvious. Managers often dislike people who push too hard for promotion, but also say that people get overlooked because they feel too modest to mention that they are interested in advancement. Managers are resistant to nagging or a sales pitch, but like to know if people have an upward trajectory in mind. Again, doing your homework is vital. How do people in your new organisation position themselves for the next advancement stage? What roles exist, and what kind of evidence and reputation would line you up for a tap on the shoulder? Here again a mentor can help you to avoid pitfalls and see the bigger picture. If you're floating the idea of a promotion, make sure you already look the part – dress like someone two rungs up the ladder.

If you're looking for a pay rise rather than a promotion, adopt a different strategy. Talking about increased responsibility may help, but it's best to argue on the basis of what more you will bring to the deal, not what you're already doing. Talk about what you have added to your role and measurable wins achieved – with tangible examples of where you have saved money, delighted customers, won business, or deputised for someone more senior. Practise by negotiating deals and discounts in your life outside work – it improves your resistance to the word 'no'.

Endings and next steps

Think about how your career conversation might conclude. You may be offered nothing, or you may be given options to consider. As your choices will have a big impact on your role, don't say 'yes' without reflection. If you don't get the top items on your list, probe alternatives such as learning opportunities, extending the range of your job, second-ments to other teams. Be ready to think on your feet if you don't get everything you want. Learn to ask, gently but very clearly, for what you want, offer options if you don't get the right offer, and always ask for a review within six months to keep the discussion open

Don't threaten to look at jobs elsewhere – that trashes your currency instantly. As soon as you threaten to leave, in the mind of many decisions-makers you're already half way out of the door. You will, effectively, be side-lined until you move out.

Keep offering potential solutions, looking for opportunities to make your job grow, and (often after asking more than once) you'll get more of what you want, shaping your job rather than rushing to the job market for a much more random result. Remember, it usually costs an employer far more to replace you than to renegotiate your career deal.

'Must do' list

Review the way you accept new challenges

- ✓ Work out how far you are contributing to the things that matter most to the organisation.
- ✓ Find out how far this is being noticed by key influencers.
- ✓ Find a mentor with the experience and objectivity to help with your development and positioning.
- ✓ Identify the main factors that get in the way of success for you, and draw up a strategy to deal with them.
- ✓ Take a fresh approach to your first appraisal meeting in your new role.
- ✓ Seek out an early opportunity for a career conversation, and prepare your suggestions with care.
- ✓ Use the RESET model to plan your next career conversation.

13

Review, build, and know when it's time to move on

'We must be willing to get rid of the life we've planned, so as to have the life that is waiting for us.' **Joseph Campbell (1991)**

This chapter helps you to:

- Avoid coasting and complacency in your new role
- Keep reviewing your career and choices
- Identify and build on your career drivers
- Refresh your career goals
- Know when it's time to renegotiate your role or move on
- Plan carefully when you consider jumping ship

As you settle into a role, it's tempting to switch on cruise control – coasting, getting on with the job and not thinking too much about your career. Think again. Don't assume you should only think about your career when you're throwing yourself at the job market.

Six-month review

Every six months, take three minutes out of your day to ask yourself three questions:

6/3/3 Question Sequence

- What have I learned in the last six months?

- How have I made a difference to the organisation that pays my salary?
- What has the last six months added to my CV?

In a fast-moving environment these three questions ensure you maintain career awareness, helping you decide where you place your attention and energy in the next six months.

Twelve-month review

Undertake a more detailed career review every 12 months or so, either on your own or with a trusted mentor or coach. This is different from the 12-month career conversation discussed in Chapter 12; instead, this is for your own development, although what you reflect on may provide evidence for conversations with others. Catalogue carefully. What have you added to your job? What new thinking have you generated or adopted? Some careers are made through managing down times and creatively squeezing thin resources. What's your contribution, and has it been noticed? Being ready to talk about what you have learned and achieved is vital for career conversations.

List high points and milestones. Look in detail at the progress you have made since taking your current job, and the things you've added to your CV. What can you do today that you couldn't do a year ago? How much change was imposed on you, and how much did you ask for? Have your last three years in work been different years, or the same year three times over? Where have you been stretched? How are you going to talk convincingly about this segment of your CV in the future when you're sitting in front of a recruiter?

Find someone encouraging who can remind you of your successes, and objective enough to ask, 'so what?' about your weaker claims. Use the **15-Minute Career Audit** below for a quick overview.

15-Minute Career Audit	
Plan	How far does your career at this point match your expectations?
Experience	How closely does your present job match the way you expected it to be?
Learning	What have you learned in the last 12 months?
Potential	How is your role likely to change in the future? How much are you likely to learn in the next 12 months?
Matching	How closely does the role you are in now match your skills and career drivers? (see below)
Motivation	How far do you feel stimulated and engaged by the work you do?
Score	What score would you give your current job out of 10, with 10 being a very strong match to your ideal role, 1 a very weak match?
Action	What steps can you take in the next three months to improve this score?

What drives you?

Looking at yourself even when you are not in transition means paying attention to your unfolding relationship with work. A career MOT, if you like. 'Job satisfaction' is high on most people's list, but it can seem vague or unrealistic. However, it is measurable, and strongly linked to our sense of engagement and loyalty. How is job satisfaction achieved?

It's highly individual, and linked to your career *drivers* – the motivating factors in a job. Some factors are external, such as the physical environment you work in or your commute to work, while others are internal, such as intellectual stimulation, variety, independence, and companionship at work. Factors that commonly reduce job satisfaction include long working hours, high-pressure work, and over-controlling bosses or cultures. Many people are motivated by the opportunity to keep learning and face new challenges.

Our drivers change over time. At the beginning of a career, we're often more focused on money, status, and the changes of progression. In the second half of a career, other things might rise in importance such as interaction with like-minded people or the chance to do meaningful work. Use the **Career Drivers** table below to score the things that matter to you today.

Career Drivers

Score your career drivers between 1 and 5, where:
- **1 = Low importance**
- **2 = Medium importance**
- **3 = High importance**

	Score
Autonomy Having some freedom to choose what you do, and how and when you perform tasks	
Change and variety A role which drives or thrives on change and offers a varied diet	
Creativity Having the opportunity to think or act creatively, sometimes operating outside the rule book	
Enterprise Creating something which didn't exist before, leading from the front	
Expertise Being recognised for particular skills or knowledge	

Influence Having opportunities to inform, apply your expertise, and influence change	
Life/work balance Work which leaves enough time and energy for you to do other important things in life	
People Enjoying the people you interact with and get to know well at work	
Purpose and meaning Work which feel like it contributes to valuable outcomes and makes a difference	
Reward Financial recognition, and the chance to increase your earnings in the future	
Stability and security Enjoying work which doesn't change too often, and long-term job security	

Look at the scores you have given to the career drivers. How many of your high scoring items feature in your current job? Job satisfaction is no mystery; for most of us it seems to happen when our career drivers are matched in work at least three days out of five.

Human beings often look for things that will make them happier, but happiness can be elusive or short-lived. A better question might be, 'what will help me grow?' A hunger for growth is one of the most frequently expressed career drivers – we like to get better at doing things, developing mastery. All jobs are exciting for a few months, simply because of their novelty. Some job components keep people energised over several years; look at what motivates you in the long term.

Career drivers focus on tasks and contexts we find congenial and stimulating. They intersect with our personal values too. For example, if working in a relationship of trust is important, this suggests core values such as integrity and enjoying the social aspects of work.

You can't expect a busy manager to instantly understand your motivators. It's your task to communicate what motivates you as part of a career conversation (see Chapter 12), and to think of ways of negotiating changes which increase the number of career drivers matched in your role.

Your learning curve

One way of reviewing progress is to think about how far your job feeds you. Are you still learning? Learning is a key career driver – many of us become dissatisfied when a role becomes routine and we're no longer learning or being challenged.

Every job can be described in terms of a learning curve. In the first weeks and months, the curve feels steep. This can feel like a panic-inducing white knuckle ride, but saying 'I'm on a steep learning curve' in fact means you're assimilating information at speed, getting there fast. A slow learning curve could mean you're not keeping up.

Most jobs are initially exciting because they are new to you. Often the expectation is that to survive in a role, you need to be a fast learner. Some jobs are mastered within two to three months, others take a couple of annual cycles. Your learning curve starts to flatten. Getting on top of the job feels at first like a welcome chance to regroup. However, even demanding roles such as sales or recruitment can become repetitive and routine. The curve can go up or down (Figure 13.1).

In the long term, learning curves don't stay flat. Soon (quicker than you might imagine), they dip, like the leaves

Figure 13.1 Where are you on the learning curve?

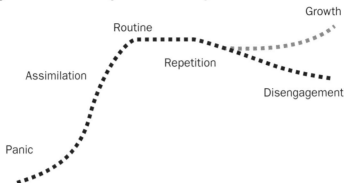

of a plant in need of water. Work becomes the 'same old same old'. A lack of learning can easily lead to resentment and disengagement.

What happens when the learning curve falls away? Without intervention, motivation starts to decline. Disengagement can easily lead to cynicism or negativity, quickly picked up by others. When you no longer find tasks challenging and the role offers few opportunities for learning, this is definitely a moment to do something which will push the curve back upwards.

The good news is, many things will do this. You might look at role extension or job sculpting, or any of the other job negotiation tools outlined in Chapter 10. Look at additional responsibilities that take you into new territory: a new project, learning new skills, or opportunities to train others or become a mentor.

Setting career goals

Career goals need to be exciting and more than a little bit brave – risk and excitement are a key part of any real challenge. Having long-term goals can help you see the key steps along the way, but the danger of ambitious career goals is that they can easily be seen as completely unattainable – too far off for you to do anything about them. We sometimes give ourselves distant targets as a way of secretly giving ourselves permission to ignore goals completely.

The first rule in goal setting is to identify the experiences you need to organise in order to create your own luck – the skills and knowledge which make you a credible candidate, the organisation names, job titles, and skills which need to appear on your CV. Discovering the most useful elements to add to the next chapter of your CV requires close attention to the marketplace and the needs of organisations. It is about the most productive use of any time you spend networking. We believe that we only need to network when job hunting, but it's also a powerful form of radar even when you're settled in a role.

The second rule is that goals are mainly achieved in small steps. An ancient urban myth now widely circulated on the Internet is the idea that your goals are more likely to be achieved if you write them down. There have been claims that this idea is based on academic research, but there is no evidence to suggest this idea has ever been proven.

People do of course reach goals, and often they do so one step at a time. They break goals down into small, achievable mini-projects - and they focus on tasks that need to be completed very soon. This means you operate with a different mindset. Rather than daydreaming your longterm future, you commit yourself to a set of actions which begin tomorrow.

Whatever stage you're at in your new role, apply this idea. As you gain ideas about how you'd like your role to develop, translate those ideas into small steps you can plan and monitor. Keep a record of what you've achieved and what you need to do next. There's always something you can do *now*, even if it's just picking up the phone to arrange a meeting with someone who can fill gaps in your knowledge.

The pathway you take to reach goals needs to be flexible, adaptive, making the best of changing circumstances. The economy reinvents itself constantly, and new kinds of jobs are being created every day. Learn the habit of curiosity – spend time regularly with people who have insights into this world of change.

Do I go or do I stay?

There's an art to knowing when it's time to move on. It's easy to feel guilt at the idea, a sense that you're betraying your employer and colleagues. Leaving a job is rarely easy. On the other hand, staying on too long can be a career-limiting action (see Chapter 11).

Whether you stay or move, do so for the right reasons. You may be clear that you need a change, and confident about throwing yourself on the market. You may have no choice in the matter because redundancy is looming. Alternatively, you may feel dissatisfied in your present situation and unsure whether you should move on to a new job or stay and try to fix the problem.

If you're starting to reach out to recruitment agencies, ask yourself a question first: 'What can I do to fix my current job?' If you are wondering what changes you can persuade your employer to make, the answer is: *often far more than you imagine*. I often meet clients who say, 'I need to be out of here by Friday', but after just a little rethinking say, 'I can make something of this'. The light at the end of the tunnel may be yours to switch on.

When you start to think about your career and take any kind of control, you see choices. Setting your own agenda helps you feel more positive about what you have to offer. Before going to the market, look at what you can fix.

Is there a good reason to stay?

Before you jump ship, explore the possibility of reshaping your job. Ask yourself: 'can my present organisation offer me the next stage in my career?' The question often doesn't occur to people who are dissatisfied in their work; they often assume they need to find a new employer. Yet it's always worth exploring whether you can fix the job you're in. It may take a lot less energy than finding a new one.

Find someone you trust well enough to talk about the issue. Focus on what's going right as well as what's going wrong. Work out what problem you're trying to fix. Are you unhappy with your role, your team, your boss, the organisation, or perhaps even your work sector? Clarity on this issue is vital, or you're trying to solve the wrong problem. For example, if you enjoy the role but don't get on with your boss, your organisation may find a new niche for your talents. If you really dislike the sector you work in, be aware of the pressure you'll experience from recruitment agencies tempting you with similar roles.

Review your career to date and see how it might find a new direction in your present organisation. Remind yourself of key evidence: what you're good at, what you've achieved, and what you might possibly offer the organisation.

Try to get an objective picture of your role, and how it might be adapted. If you move to a new role in the same organisation, does that address all the issues that cause dissatisfaction? Staying should always be a positive choice rather than the default option – telling yourself you should be grateful for job security is never more than a temporary fix.

Staying doesn't mean passively lying low. Look at renegotiating parts of your role. Making vague requests for a more interesting job doesn't help, so offer tangible initiatives as solutions that help you and the organisation (see Chapter 12 on career conversations).

Seek short-term changes – pilot schemes, attaching yourself to new teams or projects, temporary transfers – initiatives that are relatively risk-free to your organisation but of maximum value to your personal development. Ask, and be clear what you want. And if the organisation keeps saying no, or fails to respond, things are pretty clear. It's time to go.

The grass is greener . . .

If the job is really getting you down, it's tempting to jump at anything. A new job can look interesting simply because it's different. Move on because it makes sense to do so.

No matter how much you itch for change, perform due diligence on any new role that crosses your sights. In ten years you will still be explaining this job move, and you need a better explanation than 'I was desperate to get out'. A good rule of thumb is that *the attraction of the new must exceed the repulsion of the old*. In other words, the new job should be worth moving to in its own right, not because it offers an escape route.

Hunting confidentially

When you decide it's time to move on, you may need to protect your reputation by job searching with discretion. Sometimes you can be completely open with your line manager and colleagues about your intentions. This is more likely where you have been in a role for a number of years and you've had little luck identifying options for career development within the organisation.

There are many reasons why you might want to keep your job hunt confidential, particularly if you might find it difficult to find a suitable new job for some time. Your employer might be nervous about the fact that you're talking to competitors. If managers get wind of the fact that you're on the job market, they will often assume that you've broken all meaningful ties with the organisation.

This has important consequences. For one thing, you can't use social media as a showcase, because that will be noticed by many of your colleagues. You can't make a large number of direct approaches to other organisations, because your job searching can easily come up in conversation between professionals.

Don't come to the conclusion there is nothing you can do. Work with trusted external recruiters to position yourself. Get your evidence and your story straight. Seek information and ideas from people you trust, especially if they can lead you into productive conversations with other organisations. Use desk research to give you insights into new organisations without flagging up your intentions.

Prepare to leap

Before you're even tempted to jump ship, stock your lifeboat. Collect and make sense of your evidence, and get used to talking about your strengths and your achievements, as well as your reasons for wanting a change. Work out a clear career wish list and stick to it, through networking and in direct applications, so you have a clear target and strategies for aiming close to the centre.

Moving on should be about moving forwards, finding a role that is a better match for you. As we've discussed, all work is a compromise, and it's a mistake to trash your side of the bargain.

Work out the real career deal-breakers for you. Start by thinking about powerful drivers like influence, working relationships, values, trust, and your personal learning. Look thoroughly so you understand the kinds of roles available, relevant job titles, and the terms organisations use to describe top-performing workers. Perform a thorough audit of the skills, know-how, and achievements in your career kitbag, and if you go to the market, have a clear reason for doing so, emphasising the attractions of new opportunities rather than dwelling on the frustrations you will leave behind.

Shape your story

When you talk about your past to potential future employers, take care how you describe your career. You have one career, one story. Make sure it doesn't sound like a series of accidents or chance events. Don't talk about 'jumping about', false starts, or dead ends.

Tell it as a single, coherent story – a series of linked chapters which were *under your control*. Have a valid explanation for every choice you made – learning, work, even time out. Say why you made each decision, why you moved on, and what you learned from each stage.

Keep your career awareness sharp

Don't reach for the word *career* only when you're in job hunting mode. Think of it as a continually unfolding series of events, with you in charge, monitoring, adjusting, and picking your direction of travel.

Getting ahead in your new role means doing well now, and thinking ahead – accepting new challenges with your eyes open. Building your work reputation makes a difference in your first 100 days, and reshaping it may mean the difference between stagnation and growth.

Working with increased career awareness allows you to keep resetting your learning curve, avoid repeating mistakes, and to monitor where you are going in the next 18 months. It's an awareness that opens doors, and tells you when the right time comes to move up or out. Develop career awareness as a new habit – review regularly, matching your personal wish list of career drivers to the role you occupy, maintaining awareness of the career 'deal' you need now and next.

It's been said here several times: all work is a deal. Taking control means you get more out of work, in your first 100 days and way, way beyond.

'Must do' list

Review before moving on

- ✓ Look at your work history. What kind of tasks, people, and situations do you enjoy most?
- ✓ Look at yourself – list the things you do well, what you know about, and build a record of your achievements.
- ✓ Reach out to people who look as if they really enjoy their 9 to 5. Find out what jobs are really like, and how to get into them.
- ✓ Before throwing yourself at the job market, learn how to package your best evidence in a strong CV and great interview answers.
- ✓ Learn how to describe your studies and work experience in language an employer easily understands.
- ✓ Research thoroughly. Find out what organisations are most proud of, what kind of people work for them, and how they describe their most talented staff.
- ✓ Match yourself carefully to an organisation's needs when applying for advertised roles.
- ✓ Don't apologise for past decisions or jobs. Show that you've learned from every experience and applied that learning to new situations.
- ✓ Don't get locked into the idea that anything that's not entirely successful is a failure. Experiment, learn, move on.
- ✓ Practise talking about yourself well before going to a job interview.

References

Angelou, Maya (2011) *Facebook*, 4 July. Available at: www.facebook.com/
MayaAngelou/posts/10150251846629796 (accessed 16 April 2019).

Cain, Susan (2013) *Quiet: The Power of Introverts in a World that Can't Stop
Talking*. London: Penguin, p. 43.

Campbell, Joseph (1991) *Reflections on the Art of Living: A Joseph Campbell
Companion*, selected and edited by Diane K. Osbon. New York: Harper-
Collins, p. 18.

Covey, Stephen R. (1989) *The Seven Habits of Highly Effective People.*
New York: Free Press, p.101.

de Cervantes, Miguel (1615) *Don Quixote de la Mancha*, Part II, Book IV,
Chapter 38.

Drucker, Peter (1963) 'Managing for business effectiveness', *Harvard Business Review*, May. Available at: https://hbr.org/1963/05/managing-for-
business-effectiveness (accessed 24 April 2019).

Franklin, Benjamin (2013) *The Art of Virtue: Benjamin Franklin's Formula
for Successful Living*. New York: Skyhorse Publishing.

Geneen, Harold (1984) *Managing*. Garden City, NY: Doubleday, p. 274.

Gladwell, Malcolm (2006) *Blink: The Power of Thinking Without Thinking.*
London: Penguin, p. 252.

Handy, Charles (2015) *The Second Curve: Thoughts on Reinventing Society.*
London: Random House, p. 29.

Hurston, Zora Neale (1942) *Dust Tracks on a Road*. Philidelphia, PA: J. B.
Lippincott & Co., p. 142.

Institute for Employment Studies (2013) *Adult Career Decision-making:
Qualitative research*, BIS Research Paper #132. London: BIS. Available
at: www.gov.uk/government/publications/adult-career-decision-making-
qualitative-research (accessed 23 April 2019).

Manzoni, Jean-Francois and Barsoux, Jean-Louis (2002) *The Set-Up-To-Fail
Syndrome: How Good Managers Cause Great People to Fail*. Boston,
MA: Harvard Business School Press.

McCormick, Helen (2007) 'Spotlight on: First-day nerves', *Personnel Today*,
26 June. Available at: www.personneltoday.com/hr/spotlight-on-first-
day-nerves/ (accessed 27 April 2019).

Melville, Herman (1850) 'Hawthorne and His Mosses', an essay attributed to Herman Melville published in *The Literary World*, 17 and 24 August.

O'Boyle, Ed and Harter, Jim (n.d.) 'Why the onboarding experience is key for retention, *Gallup blog*. Available at: https://www.gallup.com/workplace/235121/why-onboarding-experience-key-retention.aspx (accessed 2 April 2019).

Whitehorn, Katherine (1975) 'The ten-hour week is here to stay', *The Observer*, 19 January.

Whyte, William H. (1950) 'Is Anybody Listening?' *Fortune*, September, p. 174.

Work Institute (2018) *2018 Retention Report: Truth & Trends in turnover*. Franklin, TN: Work Institute. Available at: http://info.workinstitute.com/retentionreport2018 (accessed 28 April 2019).

Index